IN SEARCH OF COMMUNITY

THE ACHIEVEMENT OF SEAN O'CASEY

IN SEARCH OF COMMUNITY

THE ACHIEVEMENT OF SEAN O'CASEY

by

HERBERT GOLDSTONE

THE MERCIER PRESS

CORK and DUBLIN

THE MERCIER PRESS
4 Bridge Street, Cork
25 Lower Abbey Street, Dublin

Printed by W. & G. Baird Ltd., Antrim

CONTENTS

Dedication

For Beth and Ann

Acknowledgement

Quotations from the writings of Sean O'Casey are taken from his works published by Macmillan and Company, London and Basingstoke.

PREFACE

In the summer of 1969 the New York Public Library purchased all of Mr. O'Casey's extant literary papers. These included essays, *marginalia,* early versions of the plays beginning with *The Silver Tassie,* the autobiographies, and a version of a very early play formerly thought lost, *The Harvest Festival* (on which the later play *Red Roses for Me* seems based). At that time much of this manuscript was completed in some form. Since then, I have had the opportunity to explore all these materials and to refer to some of them. However, none of these materials change what I am saying in this book for it is clear that the printed, stage versions represent the most important basis for consideration of the plays. But a study of the revisions makes the reasons for this all the clearer, for, as O'Casey reworked the individual plays, he tightened them structurally and verbally and made them more dramatic and poetic. For many years O'Casey may have been without access to a theatre, but as a theatrical craftsman he knew what he was doing.

Maureen Malone's book, *The Plays of Sean O'Casey* (Carbondale, Illinois, Southern Illinois University Press, 1970), which discusses the social, economic, political, and religious background of the plays, appeared after I completed much of the manuscript. While Miss Malone's book is the most complete single study of the background of the plays, most of what she presents is consistent with other sources on which I had already drawn.

Mrs. Eileen O'Casey's memoir of her life with her husband *Sean* (New York, Coward, McCann, and Geoghagen, 1972) appeared after my manuscript had gone to the publishers. Under the circumstances, regrettably, I've limited myself to brief comments on the book

2

in a long footnote–appendix in conjunction with my discussion of O'Casey's life in England (at the beginning of Section II of this book).

I am happy to take the opportunity to thank those who have provided valuable help in making this book possible. The Research Foundation of the State University of New York provided summer grants with which to initiate this book, and the Research Foundation of the University of Connecticut has provided generous typing aid. For information about O'Casey, I am particularly indebted to Mrs. O'Casey, and for encouragement and ideas at an early stage of writing to the late John Gassner who was one of the first critics to see the continuity between the early and later plays and to discern the value of the later plays. For comments and editorial aid, I am indebted to Professors Jonas Barish of the University of California at Berkeley, Harry Levin of Harvard University, and Maynard Mack of Yale University, and to two of my colleagues here at the University of Connecticut, Professors William Clark and Irving Cummings.

INTRODUCTION

If there were only two words to describe Sean O'Casey's long, stormy, and controversial dramatic career, they could certainly be *impressive* and *disappointing*.

It is impressive because of the tragic power and grim realism, especially in his first three plays, written when he was in his early forties (*The Shadow of a Gunman, Juno and the Paycock,* and *The Plough and the Stars*), which introduced into Irish drama the fascinating but stifling world of the Dublin slums O'Casey knew from personal experience as a common labourer; the great range of humour, from the frothiest slapstick to the most sardonic tragicomedy; the gallery of interesting characters, particularly the fools and childlike figures of all ages; the fantastic tonal contrasts, sometimes blatant, sometimes subtle, and often bewilderingly sudden; the eloquence and earthy vigour, as well as the richness, of the language; the varied and considerable experiments in form, especially in some of the later plays; and the force of O'Casey's compassion and yet the candour and clarity of his criticisms of his fellow men.

But equally real disappointments exist. None of the eleven plays written in his exile, beginning with *The Silver Tassie,* which was rejected by the Abbey Theatre, have achieved the success and esteem of the first three, the Dublin plays. In fact, for most critics O'Casey's whole career from his exile in 1926 to his death in 1964 seems just an anti-climax, if not a failure. For example, such a later play as *The Star Turns Red,* an expressionistic vision of a violent conflict between Fascist-clerical forces and Communist workers, has a Communist leader who on occasions resembles Superman, some wildly implausible action, and some turgid rhetoric. Moreover,

3

even the best of the later plays appear strained in some of their emotional effects and the nature of their contrasts and contain oversimplified characters and ideas.

Since O'Casey's dramatic works seem flawed, it is not surprising that critical opinion about him varies greatly. For some critics, he nevertheless remains one of the greatest figures of the modern theatre, along with Ibsen, Strindberg, Chekhov, Shaw, and Brecht. For others, he is an interesting but strictly minor figure, whose early works represent only a happy accident. And for still others, O'Casey is barely a major dramatist, possessing at most a special but limited talent.

Clearly, there is a need to try to assess O'Casey's work candidly and precisely, especially since only two of the five books so far published, David Krause's *Sean O'Casey : The Man and his Work* and Robert Hogan's *The Experiments of Sean O'Casey,* attempt any sustained critical evaluation.[1] Hogan's book, moreover, discusses form too narrowly and technically to permit much sustained evaluation. Krause's book provides an excellent overall introduction to O'Casey's plays, criticism, and autobiography, yet, it certainly leaves room for more extensive consideration of individual plays—not to mention differences of opinion or interpretation. There is a third critical book, *Sean O'Casey,* ed. Ronald Ayling, (London : Macmillan, 1969), which is a collection of essays. Though they cover most phases of O'Casey's career and some are excellent, they don't present any sustained evaluation. What should also be clear as part of such an evaluation is that O'Casey's work, despite the contradictory elements previously mentioned, represents a whole achievement. It does so not merely because of a few recurring characteristics but because of a fundamental question or theme that underlines most of the plays and makes them part of an interesting vision. When we see the plays as part of this vision, each one stands out more in its own right and its distinctive features become more apparent. This underlying question or theme is that of commitment—the compelling need that many people have to try to find some central values that give meaning to their lives. Because this need is so compelling, to discover such values is not enough. If at all possible, one tries to act upon them, and, if not, has to confront the consequences.

To ascribe such a theme to a writer many of whose greatest characters are irresponsible and amoral may seem absurd. But one distinctive feature of commitment for O'Casey is that it rests upon dynamic antithesis. For O'Casey any commitment that doesn't recognise the pull of its opposite is dubious. Consequently, even O'Casey's fools affect the commitment of other characters and vice versa. This may mean that some of the very impulses underlying the resistance to commitment, such as sheer physical enjoyment, may also become dynamic, positive forces. Nor can anything prevent fools from being passionately committed, with results that may run the gamut from the ridiculous to the pathetic.

To emphasise the central role of commitment in O'Casey's work would also seem to belabour the obvious. What theme, after all, seems more prevalent in twentieth century literature from Ibsen to Arthur Miller or Thomas Mann to Norman Mailer? But commitment for O'Casey does have a distinctive meaning that makes it a relevant focal point for a critical evaluation of his achievement. In part, this is because O'Casey, like Arthur Miller or Brecht, explores the private life in the public world. But even more important, the public world has a range of perspectives, perhaps greater than those of Brecht. These include religion, politics, sociology, economics, and aesthetics. And most important, all these perspectives, however much they differ and because they differ, affect each other. In fact, commitment for O'Casey is closely related to, if not synonymous with, community, or what Roy Harvey Pearce describes as the search for 'a moral and social order which men can accept while yet remaining sufficiently differentiated and egocentric to be aware that acceptance is an individual matter.'[2] Underlying this search is a deep conviction that the individual fulfils himself through involvement in some order larger than himself, but one which he helps fashion.

Yet O'Casey's belief in community does not mean that any existing form of community is automatically better than one that may be only visionary or difficult to achieve. The test of any form of community or commitment is whether it does justice to man's complex contradictory nature and his complex involvement with his environment. O'Casey insists that man's identity is so bound up with his environment that he is both its prisoner and yet in part its creator; that man has strong convictions and deep feelings, but that these stubbornly conflict with one another; and that he has a deep seated yearning for a better life, and yet a talent for foolish, self-destructive actions. Community may even be most significant in O'Casey's work when it does not involve a program or set of blueprints, for these might ignore massive contradictions he emphasises in human nature and society. Community may at best be an ideal illuminating, or a passionate conviction vitalising, these contradictions.

To deal with the question of commitment or community, O'Casey considers it on three planes of action : personal or private; neighbourhood or regional; and national or international. (Sometimes the neighbourhood and national may be combined by having the former a microcosm of the latter.) While these planes are distinct, they are related, for such interplay dramatises what community in its fullest implications entails. All of O'Casey's full length plays have an external or frame action which corresponds to the national (or sometimes social and national plane) and separate internal and personal actions. The external action is usually a crisis of some sort such as World War I in *The Silver Tassie,* or an occasion such as in *The Bishop's Bonfire* as the impending visit to his home town of a former local boy who has become a successful bishop. In all the plays the crisis or occasion not only exerts a significant force in its own right, but dramatically affects the personal and social actions in various ways.

By seeing how O'Casey explores commitment on these three planes, we might more clearly and justly define his dramatic achievement. Accordingly, the core of this book consists of separate chapters of analysis and evaluation of each of the plays organised in three groups.

First come the Dublin plays (1923–1926) which dramatise the complexity and difficulty of commitment in the struggle for independence from England, the most terrible historical crisis which O'Casey's generation experienced. Yet because of the suffering, waste, and powerful contradictions which the crisis accentuated, the need for community, if only as a hope, becomes important.

Next come the plays from *The Silver Tassie* (1928) to *Oak Leaves and Lavender* (1947). In these plays visionary, heroic characters try for some radical breakthrough to release valuable energies in their own lives and others around them that could provide the basis for a good life. The break-through may express itself outwardly through action and inwardly through a radical change in consciousness and perception. These energies, which might be creative, sensuous, religious, and political, are not new but were evident in the Irish even in the terrible misery underlying the Dublin plays.

Finally come the most recent plays beginning with *Cock-a-Doodle Dandy* (1949). These critically explore the possibility of realising this good life in a more limited perspective in present day Ireland, whose theocratic establishment and puritanism can damage the human spirit. There is a concluding chapter that attempts an overall synthesis and evaluation, and an appendix devoted to the one-act plays, which, although written over a period of forty years, are best appreciated when viewed together.

That commitment or community should be central to O'Casey's work is not surprising when we consider the period in which O'Casey lived in Ireland and England and some of the shaping forces in his life. Living as O'Casey did in Ireland from 1880–1926, he would certainly have become very much aware of the strong, complex feelings and issues involved in the struggle for independence. These would include the violent controversy over Parnell, the great nineteenth century nationalist leader, especially the bitter arguments about the role of the Catholic Church (opposed to Parnell because he was named in a divorce suit); the increasing militancy of the nationalist movement shown most dramatically in the Easter 1916 Rising with its considerable suffering and loss of life, and the tremendously strong passions which the uprising created among the Irish; the Black and Tan War (1919–1921) which involved bloody guerilla warfare and reprisal between Irish nationalists and the British forces; and the destructive civil war between two groups of nationalists, the Irish Republican Army and the Free State adherents, which broke out in 1922 over the signing of the peace treaty with England. (Since each of these events forms the background for one of the Dublin plays, I shall discuss them in detail in conjunction with the appropriate play.)

While O'Casey seemed less involved in political and social issues during his exile, he still maintained considerable interest in them. The Depression of the early 1930's made him conscious of the failure of English capitalism to fulfil the people's needs, as he makes clear in Volume V of his autobiography, *Rose and Crown*. The rise of German Fascism, which O'Casey also identified with authoritarian, repressive tendencies in England and Ireland, and the failure of England's Tory leaders to face up to the threat of Fascism, disturbed him deeply. Although O'Casey was not as active in movements or organisations as he had been in Ireland, he was for several years on the editorial board of the English Communist paper, *The Worker*, and considered Communism as the main hope for the ordinary man. World War II also affected him strongly because it pitted Fascism against Communism, challenged some of O'Casey's pacifist ideas, and called into question his basic national loyalties as an Irishman because he had ambivalent feelings towards both England and Ireland.

What did Communism mean for O'Casey? In discussing his beliefs with David Krause, O'Casey described Communism in these terms :

> 'Christ a Communist?' I (Krause) asked.
> 'Of course. He was. Read Shaw's great Preface to *Androcles and the Lion*. I wonder do they teach that in the schools, or in the churches? Christianity was communist from the beginning, it had to be if all men were to hold things in common and be their brothers' keepers. But you'd never know it from the way the clergy talk and act today, for they're all tactful capitalists now.'[3]

After such a mild quotation as this, it would be tempting to say that O'Casey's Communism merely represents disguised basic Christianity or his version of Fabian socialism. But this does O'Casey a real injustice, for he saw clearly the difficulties of Communism and yet some of its great possibilities. Two references in his Notebooks reveal his complex awareness of what Communism entailed. In Volume 13 (in an article on Russia) he acknowledges that in *both* England and Russia the poor can be slaves and that intellectual repression exists in both countries. Later in commenting on the Red Star of the Russian Army he asserts :

> '. . . here is a whole nation with a determination that life shall be improved at a cost : the cost of casting out the old, the conventional, the fearful, the useless, the dangerous, and any that would indifferently profit out of the brotherhood, intelli-

gence, or courage of the whole. Of course this is a one sided view of Russia, just the same as there is a one sided viewpoint wherein a distinct truth of people may be gathered together in England, Germany, Italy, and even Ireland . . ."[4]

Instead of saying, as many have, that Communism hurt O'Casey or didn't count for much, the truth might be more ambiguous. At times Communism might have helped to deepen his awareness of suffering and injustice; at other times it might have hurt him because it wasn't penetrating and forceful enough. Whatever else, we do O'Casey a great disservice to act as though he really didn't mean it when he said he was a Communist.

Besides politics, there was the cultural background, particularly the impact of the Irish Renaissance. Even if 'Renaissance' is too strong a term, we still have by any standards a richly productive period. Although I would not rule out specific formal or thematic influences, I would emphasise more strongly the inspirational force generated by the achievements and ideals of the great Irish writers. For O'Casey there could have been a strong incentive to be a writer because of the achievements of Joyce, Yeats, or Shaw, and an admiration of these figures for their independent spirit and their militant defence of the creative imagination as a significant force in national life. The Abbey Theatre, despite the lean days on which it had fallen after World War I, could also have been a source of inspiration because of its past greatness. In fact, O'Casey himself told Lady Gregory, after the Abbey had accepted *The Shadow of a Gunman,* that without the Abbey as a source of inspiration he would never have become a playwright.[5] While this is exactly what a young, unknown playwright *should* have said when discovered by the Abbey, we have enough evidence of O'Casey's candour and his admiration for Lady Gregory to accept his statement. More specifically, the particular kind of greatness of Synge, its most celebrated playwright before O'Casey, could have been important because Synge, like O'Casey, explored basic questions about the nature of belief in the lives of common people whom he found to be both comic as well as tragic, foolish and yet heroic.

Even the briefest mention of some of the details of O'Casey's life, as revealed in his autobiography, shows clearly the significance of commitment. There was the grinding poverty in which the O'Caseys, like thousands of others in Dublin, may have lived. I use the phrase 'may have' because some recent evidence suggests that O'Casey may *not* have been born in a slum but actually in a middle-class neighbourhood.[6] Yet even if this evidence is accurate, O'Casey was profoundly aware of what slum life did to human beings. Just the barest statistics make clear the terrible life of the Dublin poor in the early 1900's, perhaps the worst in any city in Europe. As David Krause points out, in 1911 Dublin's death rate was 27.6 per 1,000 compared with 27 in Calcutta and 26.3 in Moscow, which then ranked second highest in Europe.[7] While infant mortality in Dublin for the professional and middle classes was 2.5 per 1,000, among the labouring class it was 14.2 per 1,000 or almost 600 per cent greater. More than 33.9 per cent of all families in Dublin lived in only a single room, and most of these rooms were in the filthy decayed tenements that formerly had been grand eighteenth century houses.

Such poverty not only resulted in great suffering, it also pointed up terrible contrasts in human values and aspirations. Because O'Casey's sister married an insane, cruel, and selfish dreamer, she ended up a helpless wreck. O'Casey's mother also endured terrible poverty, but she still retained her courage, compassion, and an innate appreciation of beauty. O'Casey, who lived with his mother until he was almost thirty-nine, admired her tremendously for her courage, endurance, and faith, even though he felt she made too much of a virtue of Christian resignation. On the other hand, he felt indignant that his sister not only suffered so much, but had such a wasted life—a theme that permeates much of O'Casey's writing.

If religion did not exactly dominate O'Casey's life, it certainly played a prominent role. Not only was he a Protestant living in a militantly Catholic country, but he was a lower-class Protestant. He could not identify with the Protestant establishment which was middle class and aristocratic, and he had to live in an environment which certainly accentuated religious prejudice and divisions. Given such circumstances, we could expect O'Casey to criticise Catholicism strongly—and he certainly does in many of his later plays.

Still O'Casey's attitude toward Catholicism and religion itself is more complicated because religion exerted a strong positive force on him, especially in his early manhood. In part, this probably resulted from the influence of his mother, who was herself a devoted Protestant, and, as we see in his autobiography, because of O'Casey's great admiration of two local Protestant ministers for their tolerance, willingness to sacrifice themselves, and strong social conscience. Those very qualities of the ministers help define O'Casey's religion, a militant Christian socialism based on the brotherhood of man and embodied in Christ Himself whose life and sacrifice constitute a standard for judging religions. If O'Casey found most religions wanting, especially when they became formalised and were the establishment, it was not because he opposed religions, but because he felt most of them were not authentic enough. We can get some idea of how prominent a role religion played in O'Casey's young manhood from the humorous account of his behaviour in church (as recounted to David Krause by the daughter of Reverend Griffin, one of the ministers O'Casey deeply admired). As the daughter recalls, it was her father's custom at the conclusion of weekday prayer services to ask for a volunteer to lead the final prayer. At this point O'Casey (or John O'Casey as he was known then) responded :

'It was then,' she said, 'after an awkward pause while father waited for the volunteer, that my sister and I—we were girls of eight and ten—would nudge each other and whisper, "It'll be John again, he'll jump up again, and oh, he'll go on as he always does." He sat behind us and we were afraid to turn around and look, but soon we heard his voice ringing out loud and clear, in that drawling, lilting way he had of speaking. He didn't read from the prayerbook as the others did, he just made up his prayer as he went along, using some biblical passages but mostly his own words about the glory of God. As I said, at the time my sister and I joked about how he would go on and on with it, but we were silly little girls then, and when I think of it all now it comes back to me as something very moving and beautiful. He would have made a great preacher.'[8]

Actually an even more important point may not be how prominent a role religion played for O'Casey; rather, it may be, as Jack Lindsay observes, O'Casey's awareness that most of the Irish used religion as an objective correlative to articulate deep seated conflicts and problems in their lives, whether political, economic, aesthetic, or personal.[9] Therefore, whatever his own beliefs, O'Casey considered religion a significant force in his characters' lives.

O'Casey's ideal of education represents another important influence. I should say his ideal of self-education because an eye injury at an early age made it inadvisable for him to attend school. Instead, he taught himself to read and immersed himself in literature, history, and art. Having done so much on his own, it is not surprising that education for him seemed to be identified with an ethic of self-fulfilment derived largely from Ruskin whom, as we know from his autobiography, O'Casey greatly admired. In such an ethic, a liberal education in literature and the arts not only enables the ordinary person to enjoy some of the fruits of culture usually denied him, but helps him satisfy an almost religious zeal through artistic appreciation and self-development.

To education, I would add an active, practical interest in nationalist and labour movements. O'Casey was not only intellectually interested in these movements but actively involved in them as an organiser and polemicist. I am referring first to his activities in the Gaelic League over a period of years. He learned Gaelic, organised meetings and wrote articles in defence of the League. Eventually O'Casey strongly criticised the League because it too narrowly emphasised Gaelic culture as an end in itself. Nevertheless, despite these reservations, O'Casey remained active, and even the reservations themselves indicated his strong awareness of the ramifications of such a commitment.

More important than working for the Gaelic League was O'Casey's activity in the labour movement. This apparently grew directly out of his membership in the Transport Workers' Union and his great personal admiration for its president, Jim Larkin, a militant, inspirational figure in Irish labour through whom O'Casey apparently became involved in the terrible Dublin Transport Strike of 1913–1914. (I shall discuss this strike in more detail in the chapter on *The Star Turns Red* because it seems to be one of the motivating forces behind the play.) However, we can get some idea of O'Casey's intense devotion to Larkin from the way O'Casey in his first important published work, *A History of the Irish Citizens Army*, describes Larkin's appearance before a crowd :

Suddenly the window is raised, and the tense, anxious feelings of the men crowded together burst out into an enthusiastic and full-throated cheer that shatters the surrounding air, and send up into the skies a screaming flock of gulls that had been peacefully drifting along the sombre surface of the River

Liffey. Louder still swells the resonant shout as Jim
Larkin appears at the window, with an animated
flush of human pride on his strong and rugged face,
as he brushes back from his broad forehead the
waving tufts of dark hair that are here and there
silvered by the mellowing influence of Time and the
inexorable force of issuing energy from the human
structure. Again the cheers ring out, and Larkin
quietly waits till the effort to demonstrate their confidence and affection will give place to the lustful
desire to hear what he has to say to them, while
hidden under the heavy shadows of the towering
Custom House a darker column of massive con-
stables instinctively finger their belts, and silently
caress the ever-ready club that swings jauntily over
each man's broad, expansive hip.[10]

Through his association with Larkin, O'Casey became
the secretary of the Irish Citizens' Army, a labour army
organised by Larkin to defend the workers' interests and
to serve as a revolutionary force to help bring about
greatly needed economic and social changes. O'Casey
felt strongly that such an army provided the best hope
for the working man because it protected him against his
real enemy, the exploiting capitalist, who was much more
oppressive than the English. O'Casey was therefore
greatly disappointed when the Citizens' Army under
James Connolly's leadership became nationalistically
oriented and in conjunction with the Irish Volunteers, an
outgrowth of the Irish Republican Brotherhood, helped
prepare for the Easter 1916 Rising. (Actually in 1914
O'Casey had resigned from the Army because he felt
even then it was becoming nationalistic.) Although
O'Casey did not participate in the Easter Rising (despite
the fact that, as he told Lady Gregory his life was endangered at one point),[11] he felt strongly about its impact.

Disappointment may not be a strong enough term to
describe O'Casey's feelings about what happened to the

Citizens' Army, although it may help explain why he wanted to commemorate its history. Sean O'Faolain points out that O'Casey felt not only that the nationalist leaders had forgotten about labour, but that they embodied completely hostile values of middle-class, bourgeois capitalism and clericalism :

> Sean O'Casey's plays are thus an exactly true statement of the Irish Revolution whose flag should be, not the tricolour, but the plough and the stars of the labouring classes. We must, finally, understand that the class that thus came to power and influence was not a labouring class; the most able among them changed their nature by changing their place in life —they graduated, rapidly into petit bourgeois, middlemen, importers, small manufacturers, thus forming a new middle class to fill the vacuum formed by the departure or depression of the alien middle class. These men, naturally, had had very little education, and could have only a slight interest in the intellectuals' fight for liberty of expression. They were ordinary, decent, kindly, self-seeking men who had no intention of jeopardising their mushroom-prosperity by gratuitous displays of moral courage. In any case, since they were rising to sudden wealth behind protective tariff-walls, they had a vested interest in nationalism and even in isolationism. The upshot of it was a holy alliance between the Church, the new businessmen, and the politicians.[12]

This quotation is very important. It helps explain O'Casey's critical treatment of the Irish nationalist crises in the Dublin plays (and why the flag of the Citizens' Army, the *Plough and the Stars*, should be the title of his greatest play). It may also make clearer some of the reasons for his exile; and it illuminates his last plays which deal with a contemporary Ireland very much like that which O'Faolain describes.

O'Casey's long exile in England reveals still other facets of commitment. During the exile, which was spent largely in Devon with his wife, the Irish actress Eileen Carey, and his family, O'Casey apparently lived a much quieter and happier life than he had ever known in Ireland. The exile began in 1926 after the celebrated riots in the Abbey over O'Casey's alleged attacks on Irish patriotism and morality in *The Plough and the Stars*. For O'Casey, the riots represented all too clearly the repressive, divisive forces of puritanism and factionalism which he felt would stifle artistic creativity and reform in Ireland, and which were one consequence of the triumph of the nationalists, whether Free Staters or Republicans, in the struggle for independence. He also felt that these forces could frustrate his own desire for a free personal life so long denied him because of his poverty and involvement in various Irish causes. I am not trying to determine whether O'Casey should have gone into exile, because this is a question *after* the fact, but only to point out that the exile itself and O'Casey's strong feelings about it, as expressed in his autobiography, accentuate the importance of commitment. As important as the exile itself was O'Casey's insistent, anguished concern to justify it.

Finally, I would emphasise the strong personal affection which O'Casey showed for those whom he greatly loved and admired. Most important was his mother, then Jim Larkin, his sister, and perhaps Lady Gregory, to whom he remained loyal despite his bitter feelings toward the Abbey for rejecting *The Silver Tassie*. At a greater remove were such other figures as the Reverend Griffin, and the Catholic theologian, Professor Walter MacDonald,[13] who suffered neglect and bitter disappointment because of his unsuccessful efforts to question church dogma. I am not trying to determine which people were closest to O'Casey, but only to emphasise the force and persistence of his devotion, his fierce ardour, and unfailing sympathy. For O'Casey these people embodied an ideal against which he measured all others, himself included. If the judgment was often severe, this in itself indicated the great value which such an ideal represented for him.

More effective than any mere summary could be is this vivid account of O'Casey by the prominent Irish historian Desmond Ryan, who remembered him as a young man :

Once Seamus and I left Mount Street and found ourselves in a Drumcondra Sinn Fein club. . . . On the back benches sat Sean O'Casey, then much swayed by memories of Wolfe Tone, Robert Emmet, and especially Shane the Proud's head spiked on Dublin Castle in the days of Good Queen Bess, this last event in those days a burning and personal grief of his; it jostled bitter phrases from Mitchel and Lalor's most urgent calls to revolt on the eve of Forty-Eight in all Sean's speeches.

Sean O'Casey sits in silence, at the back of the hall during the lecture, a dour and fiery figure swathed in labourer's garb, for he works on the railways just then. His neck and throat are bound in the coils of a thick white muffler, and he looks like a Jacobin of Jacobins as his small, sharp and red-rimmed eyes stab all the beauty and sorrow of the world. He speaks first, and very fluently and eloquently in Irish; then launches out into a violent Republican oration in English, stark and forceful, Biblical in diction with gorgeous tints of rhetoric and bursts of anti-English Nationalism of the most uncompromising style. He will have none of the Socialists who have turned in to heckle the lecturer and he rends them savagely and brushes their materialism aside. Yes, he reminds them, when roused by his sharp words, they murmur interruptions taunting him with the poverty and degradation of the Dublin workers, there is all that in life. Half to himself he speaks, lowering his voice to an intense whisper, but there is something else; joy. He speaks the word, and his tone gives a meaning to it even as he sinks down into silence on the bench, his fierce small head an angry star over all the others in the rear. Walter Carpenter rises and would argue with him, serious anger a-gleam in two grey bespectacled eyes. Walter is a leading Socialist propagandist, a most humourless and self-sacrificing man who walks in from Dunleary each night from home to his meetings in the city; he has ruined his worldly prospects for his beloved Red Flag and all but lost his business on the head of it. He is to be heard at the Socialist Party of Ireland, announcing solemnly that there will be a social followed by a supper, a cold supper, comrades, and you are all earnestly invited to attend and see how Socialists be'ave themselves. His voice moans a reproach and an argument to Sean O'Casey. The fierce star at the rear becomes a soaring and hissing comet : O'Casey rises in a fury and growls in Irish like a thunderstorm that he wishes no Englishman to teach him. Sean strides through the door with flames in his eyes and his fists clenched. A translation of his farewell reaches Walter, whose accents grow more and more suited to a wake. With a sob in his keen, he wails; 'I 'ope some one will go out after that misguided individual who 'as rushed out eaten up with radical 'atred and tell him for Gawd's sake, that I am not an Englishman but a Scotchman, and that I 'ad the honour to drop a tear in the grive of Charles Stewart Parnell.' Soon Sean O'Casey fell under the spell of Larkin and became as fierce a Labourist as he had been a physical-force Republican, still suspicious of the Socialist, and perhaps finding models for his Covey in his *Plough and the Stars*. The pages of Larkin's *Irish Worker* carried articles from his pen, all remarkable in their style and power with an independent outlook struggling through the over-fine writing and exotic wordiness. . . . Yet that night in Drumcondra who could suspect he would yet voice the darkest depths of slum-land and the agony of unsuspected years of turmoil and terror? As O'Casey strode beside his pipers' band or spoke in the clubs there was a force and character about him even if you thought he was a crank, a fanatic, a man whose mind has room for only one idea at a time. In private he had a courtesy and simplicity.[14]

Nor does this passage merely represent Ryan's own subjective reaction. Even the most cursory glance at O'Casey's early writing, collected by Robert Hogan in *Feathers from the Green Crow*, as well as the text of the unpublished play *The Harvest Festival* (which, as mentioned, was until quite recently thought to be lost) confirms the same impressions. The play in particular stands out for it portrays the heroic efforts of a young labour leader (similar to O'Casey himself) to better conditions for his men. Not only does the leader concern himself about economic realities, but he has a vision of a fuller life that includes religion, art, and creative personal fulfilment, all of which could enrich the life of the ordinary person. Not content with just articulating these beliefs, the young leader dies in leading his men in a bitter strike.

This brief description of the play and Ryan's reminiscence make clear the strong connection between conviction and action, the insistence that commitment is not merely intellectual and serious but also instinctive and joyous, and that it necessarily involves both the public and private life, however much they may conflict. In fact, the very strength of the conflict asserts the value of both forces and their indissoluble connection.

THE COMMUNITY OF SUFFERING

THE SHADOW OF A GUNMAN

The first of the famous Dublin plays, *The Shadow of a Gunman* (given its premiere at the Abbey Theatre, April 1923) fittingly introduces us to a distinctive world that we also find in *Juno and the Paycock* and *The Plough and the Stars*. This is a world in which significant crises in the Irish struggle for independence are experienced not by great heroes and patriots such as those in Yeats' 'Easter 1916' but by ignorant and poor Dublin tenement dwellers bewilderingly caught up in these events. By presenting Irish history from this new perspective of the poor, anti-heroic Irish, O'Casey exposed many myths about romantic Ireland that the Irish in the first flush of their independence had conveniently forgotten or—what is worse—conveniently exaggerated. For this reason alone the three plays are important because they portray these significant national events freshly and realistically.

But the importance of the Dublin plays far transcends the particular. That is because they explore basic conflicts and contradictions in the common people and their society as they are involved in the profound suffering of historical change which characterises much of the twentieth century. In these crises O'Casey sees many of the forces and character traits that reveal the Irish and, by implication, other common people at their worst—prejudiced, selfish, irresponsible, and cowardly. Yet he also shows them at their best—honest, courageous, loving, and deeply realistic. The Dublin plays attack most of the Irish because they live such shabby lives, but they also exalt some of them for heroic qualities of spirit. And whether O'Casey's Irish are at their best or their worst, they are so alive and humorous that from 1923 on they have continued to captivate theatre audiences who may have only the vaguest knowledge of romantic Ireland and the Dublin tenements.

In *The Shadow of a Gunman,* the national crisis is the terrible Black and Tan War of 1919–1921. During this bloody time there were recurring raids involving Irish Republicans split into small, highly effective guerrilla groups of gunmen operating through ambush and bombing and special British forces assigned to the Irish police.

These British forces included the Regular Army (called the Tommies) and two special forces : the Auxiliaries, consisting of former officers, assigned to the Royal Irish Constabulary; and another made up mostly of unemployed former private soldiers. From this second group who wore khaki coats with black trousers and caps originated the name of the Black and Tans, and once this group came to Ireland they developed a distinct reputation for cruelty which left its mark on this phase of the nationalist crises. The play, as a matter of fact, takes place in May 1920 when such raids were at their height and consequently most of the Irish lived in abject terror, especially in a tenement building where such a raid endangered many lives.[15] In this atmosphere O'Casey presents a series of events which under ordinary circumstances would be harmless and amusing—as they are in the play for the first half (Act I). These events centre around the mistaken notion of a group of tenement dwellers that Donal Davoren, a poet with a Shelleyesque vision of beauty and poetic inspiration, who is temporarily living with a friend, Seumas Shields, is really an Irish Republican terrorist in hiding. Actually Davoren is staying with Shields, a disorganised, fearful one-time nationalist, because he thinks he will find peace and quiet that will enable him to write. But such is not the case. The neighbours make their mistake because of cowardice, fear, ignorance, and highly romanticised ideas of love and heroism. Donal, in turn, encourages them because this flatters his vanity and brings him the love of Minnie Powell, an attractive, courageous but naive girl who idolises him as a great national hero. In Act II, however, the entire complexion of events changes drastically when the British soldiers, the Tommies, raid the tenements in search of bombs and gunmen. This raid gives the play the motion and force of a shattering explosion in which only the pieces are left.

It so happens that a suitcase left in Seumas' room by one of his employees, who was a real gunman, actually contains bombs. During the raid Minnie offers to hide them in her room because she wants to protect Davoren. In addition, she naively assumes that the British would be too gentlemanly to search her room. Nor do Davoren and Shields object because they are so terrified. The British discover the bombs and arrest Minnie. When out of loyalty to Donal she excitedly expresses Republican sympathies, the British shoot her dead. In the end Donal stunningly realises that his responsibility for Minnie's death makes him only a Shadow of a Gunman. On the other hand, Seumas, who is almost as guilty as Donal, stubbornly disclaims any responsibility for Minnie's death.

The word *responsibility* is crucial in this play and in *Juno* and *The Plough and the Stars* because it reveals some of the deepest implications of O'Casey's portrayal of the Irish during the Black and Tan War and the two other crises. Through skilful contrasts in characterisation between the men and women and between individual men and individual women, O'Casey shows three distinct, but related, views of responsibility.

The first and most important is complete denial. This denial is evident in the pervasive desire of all the male characters to avoid pain at any cost. Harmless, innocuous Mr. Gallagher wants the Irish Republican Army, which was then just beginning to set up rudimentary law courts,[16] to keep the children playing in the hallway of his apartment from bothering him with their noise. That the Irish Republican Army might have more important things to do, or that the children might have no other place to play, completely escapes him. Truculent, alcoholic Adalphus Grigson is a prosperous well-fed Orangeman, in contrast to his wife, who is emaciated and exhausted from catering to him. Even more important, Grigson is a crude opportunist out to protect his own skin during the raid. He shamelessly cites scripture to justify his every move, regardless of how contradictory it is, and he boasts of resisting the British, when actually he quaked in his boots. O'Casey ridicules Grigson so strongly because he is so selfish and bourgeois-oriented and of course is a member of the hated Orange! A third sad case is Tommy Owens, who uses hero worship and flag waving to conceal his terrible fear. Tommy brazenly identifies himself with all the great Republican heroes and lives vicariously through their exploits. At the same time he can also outdo everyone else in parroting all the popular nationalist slogans. Drunk on rhetoric, he uses it to insulate himself from the terror.

While the rationalisations of Mr. Gallagher, Grigson, and Tommy are obvious, those of Seumas Shields are more subtle and interesting. They show what can happen to an able and intelligent person when he dissipates his energies and is paralysed by fear. Seumas is an educated person who at an earlier time taught Gaelic in night school and was an ardent patriot. When he began to realise how uncritically his comrades welcomed violence as a romantic ideal and how foolishly they attributed all of Ireland's difficulties to English domination, he became disaffected. While Seumas may be rationalising, these criticisms could be legitimate, since, as I pointed out, O'Casey himself had said the same things when he saw Larkin's labour army transformed by Republicans. Seumas, however, has found nothing to take the place of his nationalist faith. Instead, he has become a shabby suspender salesman who has ingeniously projected his own faults onto his countrymen. Worst of all, he conceals his fears by transforming them into supernatural portents that justify religious orthodoxy. In this way he has been able to dissociate himself from any responsibility for his actions. His cowardice is more pervasive than that of Tommy or Grigson because he has some rational superstructure on which to ground it and the intelligence to defend himself against attack. In portraying Seumas, O'Casey is exploring another pervasive theme, the human waste which results from these crises, for Seumas is a caricature of his former self.

Donal's retreat from responsibility takes place through his art. Why, he asks himself, should he endure the pain of living in an ugly, real world when by all rights he should be free to live in his own created world of ideal beauty. While the terror is going on, he looks only for peace and quiet to permit him to write poetry. Donal sincerely believes in his art, for he has suffered personal deprivation to continue writing. Sensitive and intelligent, he recognises that Minnie is not just another pretty girl but a potentially creative person who simply hasn't had a chance to develop herself. Donal has, nevertheless, exaggerated his suffering and pities himself too much (he is always quoting Shelley, 'the pain, the pain'). Nor will he admit that, despite all his talk about confronting suffering, he himself looks for the easy way out. When Minnie mistakes him for a gunman, he can't resist the temptation to capitalise on her error. In all fairness to Donal, I admit that at this point there seems to be little danger and he does weigh the consequences. But Act II is another story. When Minnie comes to his room and offers to take the bombs away, he simply yields out of crass fear. For this reason he is more directly responsible for her death than Seumas, though less ravaged by the life he has led.

In striking contrast to the men who flee from responsibility and pain are the women who welcome it, even exult in it. Mrs. Henderson, a burly, good-natured woman, fights the British troops singlehanded during the raid, and Minnie, of course, gives her life for Ireland.

Besides being brave, the women are generous and loving. They all involve themselves with a man from whom they ask little, if anything, in return. What is more, Minnie, in particular, shows real independence of spirit and self-confidence. Although she has spent her life in the dreary tenements, she asks no one for help and is not afraid to make decisions.

Admirable as the women are, they do cause *some* of the damage. Admittedly, they bear less responsibility than the men because they have been victimised more by their environment. The women simply don't think carefully or critically enough and, therefore, act rashly. They do so, not because of stupidity, but because of too narrow a preoccupation with their own life, however unsatisfying it may be.

While Mrs. Grigson bravely endures suffering, she restricts her entire life to worrying about her oafish husband and undoing the damage he causes. As a loving, compassionate woman, she must have someone to whom she can devote herself, and Grigson at least satisfies this need. It is also true that her environment has victimised her because, with her range of experience, she can't expect much out of life. But her problem is not this simple. Mrs. Grigson accentuates her own misery because she overvalues respectability and status, which she identifies with her husband. Consequently, she lets him dominate her. If, however, she could accept her husband more for what he is, she might do somewhat better. A more important limitation is that—at least until the end of the play—her love seems narrow and useless. Concerned only about her husband, she ignores many others who obviously are suffering much more than he is.

Minnie is simply too naive a romantic. Having read Sir Walter Scott, she believes that gunmen such as Donal are great romantic heroes whom she should idealise. Minnie's environment bears some responsibility, for, as Donal has pointed out to Seumas, she has the native intelligence and taste to find a better life for herself. Yet

Minnie acts as she does because she is warm-hearted and impulsive; it is not her fault that Donal should treat her so shabbily.

But, admirable as Minnie is, she bears some share of the blame, for her romantic hero worship does satisfy some egotistical needs. She looks up to Donal as a hero because she wants such a hero for herself. Nor is she so desperate that she has to live in a world of fantasy rather than one of reality. Yet, I don't wish to belabour this point because Minnie's death is moving and she is sympathetic.

Admittedly *The Shadow of a Gunman* shows some clear signs of being an early play. Leaving a suitcase full of bombs in Seumas' room seems too clumsy a device to bring off the tragedy. Once we learn at the end of Act I that McGuire, the man who had left them, was an actual gunman shot by the British, it is obvious what will happen. Nor is the contrast between McGuire, the real gunman, and Donal, the shadow of a gunman, sustained enough to be effective, since McGuire is never shown in any real danger. Still another limitation is that, while Seumas and Donal are chattering away to conceal their fear, the first part of Act II seems to drag. After all, it is not easy to be interesting, when Donal takes himself so seriously as a Shelleyesque poet and Seumas as a great Irish pundit.

If, however, *The Shadow of a Gunman* betrays its youth, the crime is not a major one. O'Casey compensates by vividly portraying striking contradictions within his characters. On the one hand, they have an ingenous vitality. In the most recent production I have seen of this play (at the Drama Centre in London) this vitality was evident just in the fast pace of the action and in the way people kept insistently breaking in upon Donal and Seumas. Before we know it, the landlord, McGuire, Mrs. Henderson, Mr. Gallagher, Tommy, and Minnie have all barged in without the slightest hesitation, and each makes his demands without any self-consciousness or restraint. Yet, on the other hand, these characters waste vitality. The women, as indicated, waste their love on the men; the men dissipate their energies in cowardice. Seumas works hard in denouncing his countrymen, while Grigson seems almost irrespressible in browbeating everyone around him. Such vitality, together with intelligence, courage, and compassion could make responsibility meaningful. But, when combined with fear and deception, it can be dangerous and destructive.

While all the men have a talent for deceiving themselves and others, Tommy Owens and Seumas seem the most energetic and ingenious. Tommy can make himself believe almost anything to bolster his ego and conceal his cowardice. He can imagine himself able to consort with heroes, to be deeply frustrated because he has not been asked to die for his country, and to be supremely tolerant and understanding as a trusted confidant. Carried away by all the sentimental stock phrases and slogans of the day, Tommy shifts from one heroic pose to another. When Minnie tries to stop him from reciting an Irish patriotic ballad, with tears in his eyes he turns to Donal and remarks that he would die for Ireland. When Donal tries to cheer him up by reminding him that 'They also serve who only stand and wait', Tommy dramatically changes his pose to that of the chauvinistic patriot:

> I'm bloody well tired o' waitin'—we're all tired o' waitin'. Why isn't every man in Ireland out with the I(rish) R(epublican) A(rmy)? Up with the barricades, up with the barricades; it's now or never, now an' for ever, as Sarsfield said at the battle o' Vinegar Hill...[17]

Seumas' defences against reality are more varied than those of Tommy. They are all truculent and aggressive as though it were inconceivable he could be wrong about anything. Seumas has a real talent for attacking his fellow countrymen just where he himself is most vulnerable. After Donal ridicules him for not having been ready to keep an appointment, Seumas violently criticises the Irish for being lazy. The most fearful evidence of Seumas' 'know it all' attitude, however, comes out in his vicious personal attacks, particularly on Minnie. Seumas warns Donal about getting involved with Minnie because she is just a cheap, vulgar, sentimental girl who merely wants a romantic thrill in war time :

> . . . An' what ecstasy it ud give her if after a bit you were shot or hanged; she'd be able to go about then —like a good many more—singin', 'I do not mourn me darlin' lost, for he fell in his Jacket Green'. An' then, for a year an' a day, all round her hat she'd wear the Tricoloured Ribbon O, till she'd pick up an' marry someone else—possibly a British Tommy with a Mons Star. An' as for bein' brave, it's easy to be that when you've no cause for cowardice; I wouldn't care to have me life dependin' on brave little Minnie Powell—she wouldn't sacrifice a jazz dance to save it.

This speech is grimly ironical not only because Minnie's bravery later saves Seumas' life, but also because of the terrible waste of intelligence and imagination it reveals. Seumas describes what probably *did* happen in many cases, but he is completely wrong about Minnie. He has no idea that he hates Minnie so much because she passionately believes in the very ideals which he himself because of cowardice has now abandoned.

After this evidence of Seumas' cruelty, we would not be surprised if O'Casey were very hard on his characters, but actually he shows much compassion, particularly evident in his refusal to oversimplify the characters' responsibility for what has occurred. The last episode, which presents the reactions to Minnie's death, stands out because it crystallises the meaning and force of the play.

Seumas' first reaction to the news is one of cowardly

defensiveness : if Davoren does not calm down, the British will hear the noise and raid again. When Donal tries to get Seumas to admit some responsibility for what has occurred, Seumas can still cleverly resist. He does so by using his intelligence and superstition to insulate himself from any feelings he may have. By shrewdly pointing out that Minnie freely chose to take the bombs to her room, he can outface Donal and ignore any other consideration. He also has superstition to protect him. 'I knew,' he mutters, 'something 'ud come of the tappin' on the wall.' Mrs. Grigson's reaction, in contrast, expresses such greater ignorance, but it also reveals an elemental understanding of what has occurred. She has no idea why Minnie or anyone else acted as she did or what responsibilities, if any, the nationalists may have had. Yet she does see Minnie's death in its most terrible, final implications : '. . . The ambulance is bringin' her to the hospital, but what good's that when she's dead ! Poor little Minnie, poor little Minnie Powell, to think of you full of a life a few minutes ago, an' now she's dead !'

Although Donal's reactions, in contrast, reveal greater shock and personal involvement, they lack Mrs. Grigson's unself-conscious compassion. After Donal hears the news of Minnie's death, he begs Seumas to understand how responsible they both are for the death. Admittedly, such a reaction is defensive since he is projecting some of his own guilt onto Seumas. When Seumas remains unaffected by his entreaties, Donal, however, accepts his own responsibility :

> Ah me, alas ! Pain, pain, pain ever, for ever ! It's terrible to think that little Minnie is dead, but it's still more terrible to think that Davoren and Shields are alive ! Oh, Donal Davoren, shame is your portion now till the silver cord is loosened and the golden bowl be broken. Oh, Davoren, Donal Davoren, poet and poltroon, poltroon and poet !

Because he has been deeply moved he judges himself

rigorously and painfully. But even at this moment, as his self invocation reveals, self-pity and self-concern still obtrude.

The last episode shows the first step that Donal has taken under the shattering impact of Minnie's death, and how this sets him apart from all the other men and perhaps the women. Mrs. Grigson's speech, however, reminds us by contrast how large a gap exists between Donal's self-conscious awareness and her own more compassionate response. At the same time Seumas remains the strongest force of all since he is so stubborn. O'Casey does not dissolve the play into sentimental optimism or pessimism; he portrays pointedly and modestly the beginning of a more complex sense of responsibility—but *only* the beginning; one made all the more poignant because, if it had come earlier, the great human waste in Minnie's death might have been averted.

JUNO AND THE PAYCOCK

We can all too easily both underrate and overrate *Juno and the Paycock,* the brilliantly amusing but sometimes heart-rending portrayal of the disintegration of a Dublin tenement family, the Boyles. We can underrate the play if we merely think of it as a lively, free-wheeling comedy that suddenly takes a tragic turn at the end. While in some respects the tragedy is forced and sudden, the comedy remains an integral part of O'Casey's vision in which folly, selfishness, and moral chaos have grim, tragic consequences. On the other hand, we overrate the play if we assert that its affirmation of responsibility and elemental family love, embodied in Mrs. Boyle (Juno), is as sustained or powerful as the irresponsibility and selfishness embodied in Boyle himself (the Paycock). In between these two extremes of judgment, we can still appreciate *Juno* as one of O'Casey's best plays, if only for Boyle himself, one of the greatest comic creations in modern drama and the supreme embodiment of the forces of egotism so important in the play.

Like *The Shadow of a Gunman, Juno* also takes place against a war background in which terror and ambush are all too common. This time, however, instead of fighting a common enemy, the English, Irishmen are fighting each other in a civil war. Nor would the civil war seem to make sense because it broke out right after the Irish had signed a peace treaty with England that gave them dominion status and considerable self-determination. But since the treaty did require an oath of allegiance to the British crown, though nominal, and it did not apply to the six counties of Northern Ireland, it did not embody the objectives to which the nationalists had pledged themselves, an Irish Republic and a Republic of all of Ireland. In addition, as historians point out,[18] there were other, more complex reasons having to do, among other things, with the conduct of the negotiations, and poor communication between the Irish delegates in London and their government in Dublin. Whatever the case, a sizable number of nationalists, led by De Valera and much of the Irish Republican Army, felt impelled to oppose the treaty and to refuse to take the required oath of allegiance to King George V. Actually, the reasons are less important than the climate of opinion created by the causes and course of the war.

For the average person and indeed many Irish leaders the causes were vague, since they were complex and ambiguous, despite much debate in the Dáil Eireann (the Irish parliament). In fact, the average person couldn't believe there were any good reasons to explain the tragedy. After all, the very leaders supporting the treaty (who constituted the Irish Free State), insisted that the treaty really did embody, potentially, the Republican ideals to which both sides earlier had pledged themselves. Such an ambiguous situation in which people could either affirm or deny the reality of the war strengthened the Republicans in their conviction that if only the people knew the facts, they would support them. Therefore, the Republicans, though losing, also felt impelled to pursue their cause. Any deviations from their camp would have been considered treasonous.

If the causes were ambiguous, the nature and course of the war were not. It was brutally clear : there were raids and reprisals, similar to the Black and Tan terror, but probably much more destructive. Dorothy MacArdle[18] estimates that at one time there were 15,000 political persons in Free State jails; how many under Republican confinement she does not say. This is not to mention the executions, injuries, and deaths by ambush, on both sides. O'Casey in Volume III of his autobiography describes one such horrifying incident, which makes anything in

Juno tame by comparison.[19] This incident involves a young Republican bomb thrower who, after a long, hectic chase, is cornered by three Free Staters led by a Colonel who as a sergeant had been one of the Republicans' buddies in fighting the Black and Tans. To the very end, the bomb thrower really can't believe what is going to happen to him :

—Jesus ! whimpered the half-dead lad, you wouldn't shoot an old comrade, Mick !
The Colonel's arm holding the gun shot forward suddenly, the muzzle of the gun, tilted slightly upwards, splitting the lad's lips and crashing through his chattering teeth.
—Be Jesus ! We would, he said, and then he pulled the trigger.[20]

A war which was so poorly understood and yet so violent, so secret and yet so open since people in the same building could be killing each other, could produce national schizophrenia. For one had to be prepared to live simultaneously in radically different worlds, each of which seemed both real and unreal.

Besides the similar background of terror, *Juno* also has a plot structure that depends upon a 'gimmick' and sudden changes of fortune. This 'gimmick' is an unexpected legacy that dramatically changes the lives of the Boyles, who have been existing in rancour and squalor. Captain Boyle, or the Paycock, is a lazy, irresponsible boaster, even more ingenious in his defences against reality than Seumas. Mrs. Boyle, or Juno, is a shrewd, realistic, and compassionate woman. But she too easily equates her realism with economic security and lets middle-class, or lace-curtain, gentility dominate her. Mary, the daughter, is an intelligent, idealistic girl who, like Minnie, envisions a nobler life than that of the slums. Her problem is that she likewise identifies this life with middle-class gentility, although for different reasons than her mother. As for Johnny, her brother, he is a disillusioned Irish Republican Army veteran who has informed on one of his comrades. (About his connection with the play, more later.) Carried away by their expectations, the Boyles plunge into debt and put on absurd, middle-class airs. When it turns out that the law clerk (Mary's fiancé) who drew up the will made it too ambiguous, the roof falls in on the Boyles. Mary is deserted by her fiancé after she has become pregnant; Juno, together with Mary, walks out on Boyle because he has known for some time that the inheritance was out of the question. Boyle, like Seumas, stubbornly refuses to accept any responsibility for what has happened and retreats into a drunken stupor; and Johnny is killed by his Republican comrades in reprisal.

While Johnny's death certainly has no direct connection with the inheritance fiasco, his disillusionment and betrayal do. Although Johnny does not make his motives too clear, apparently as a mere boy he joined the Irish Republican Army (or a youth organisation with similar purposes) in 1916 because of confused motives. He believed in the cause, though how deeply or knowingly is difficult to tell, and he apparently had the support of his parents and neighbours. Despite the fact that he was wounded in the hip and lost his arm, he remained loyal to the cause for several years. As he remarks to his mother, 'a principle is a principle'. At the time the play begins, however, he seems to have reached the breaking point because, like all the other characters, he found himself undermined by an insidious, corrosive force. This force, to use Boyle's great malapropism, is a 'state o' chassis' or moral chaos, brought on by successive national crises and the stifling, divisive environment. The many conflicting loyalties undermined by the years of fighting, the failure of the average person to understand the issues of the civil war, and the enervating effects of the prejudice and poverty in the environment have demoralised the characters. Consequently, they desperately need something that will provide some structure to their lives.

For them conformist pressures or appearances such as material status seem to be the answer. Of course they aren't, since they are just a projection of the most elemental selfish needs. As a result, people have become even more confused, self-centred, and irresponsible than before, though this may not be apparent to them.

Or another way to describe what has happened is to say that there is the appearance of community rather than the substance, and that the need even for appearance is important; but that the consequences for settling for appearance and middle-class materialism are disastrous, at least for the Boyles. When we further remember that O'Casey (as O'Faolain pointed out), associates these particular values with nationalism, we can beter understand why the play has such serious consequences.

While the 'state o' chassis' affected every one—and the variety of ways is what is interesting in the play—it affected Johnny Boyle the most. He is traumatised, fearful, reduced to a shell of a person. Although O'Casey gives us very little to go on, I think we can infer that Johnny simply couldn't sustain his Republican convictions. This would have been difficult for anyone, but was accentuated for him because his neighbours and parents, whose support he needed, came to regard the Republicans as 'Diehards'. (This apparently was the state of affairs just before the play opens.) As a result, Johnny had nothing to believe in and, in bitterness and desperation, began to hate those forces that made him what he was, his family and the Irish Republican Army. He fights bitterly with his father who epitomises the worst in his family and informs on one of his comrades, his neighbour, Robbie Tancred. Having betrayed Tancred, Johnny becomes even more self-centred because now he lives in utter fear of his life. Except for arguing with Boyle, he has no defenses, so that he is reduced to letting his mother treat him like a sick child.

Although Johnny does not appear in very many scenes, he shows us to what desperate lengths people can go when at best they have only basic selfish feelings to sustain them, and at worst, they begin to destroy even these. The fact that Johnny does embody so clearly the confusion and narrow self-interest with which the play concerns itself may explain why O'Casey, during rehearsals, used to refer to *Juno* as the play about Johnny Boyle.[21]

Mary Boyle's problem is one of shallowness of belief. It is true that Mary can envisage a better life than that of the tenements and she is determined to try to attain this in some way. Active in her union, she supports her fellow workers when they go out on strike, even though her family objects and she jeopardises her own job. Through Bentham, she hopes to create a more interesting and dignified life than that of her family or neighbours, which she scorns as materialistic. She simply doesn't see that she also accepts appearances as an end-all, except that for her they exist on a higher social plane. Besides being victimised by her environment, Mary romanticises or idealises her own self interest and vanity. Ironically, because Mary is finer grained than most of the others in her environment, she indulges herself more subtly.

Common sense realism may have its virtues, but *Juno* reveals that it may also be foolish and destructive. Basically generous and compassionate, Juno has worn herself out assuming the major family responsibilities which Boyle has simply ignored. How much waste this involves is clear from one of the stage directions which emphasises that under other circumstances she could have been talented and still good looking. Although she has been heroic, she has also been somewhat foolish. Not only has she let Boyle take advantage of her by being so shiftless, but she may even prefer such a situation. In this way she can exult her importance by exposing Boyle for being so lazy and tricky. But even more important evidence of her foolishness is that, like Mother Courage, Juno simply doesn't realise that she has let the very conditions of life which have victimised her become her ultimate standard of value. Consequently, once Boyle seems to be getting the inheritance, Juno encourages him to be a proper middle-class husband to whom appearance and material security mean everything, and she disclaims any responsibility for what he does.

For Boyle such a disclaimer does not matter. But by accepting such ultimate values, Juno does hurt Johnny. Under the influence of the first, she may have encouraged Johnny to enlist without realising how shallow such motivation actually was. Then, when the going was rough, she ridiculed Johnny for being an impractical diehard, unaware that this could only make his plight all the worse. Nor does she see that both her approval and disapproval of Johnny's patriotism represent two sides of the same coin. For all her sympathy, Juno remains powerless to help Johnny because she can't understand what happened to him.

If Juno bears considerable responsibility for what occurs, Boyle still bears the most precisely because he is so callous and self-centred. Throughout the play he thinks only of himself, even if it is just to cheat his parastic buddy, Joxer Daly, out of breakfast sausage or to fancy himself a successful business man. As his nickname 'Paycock' suggests, he struts around, enthralled with himself, ever on the alert to wheedle his way out of work and to boast about his imagined exploits. Certainly Boyle's behaviour largely results from his character; how could he be otherwise? Nevertheless, the squalid tenement and the chaos create a strong temptation to escape, if possible. And Boyle has a great talent for such escape. He can shamelessly live off Juno when this is possible; he can always enjoy himself because he has vitality and zest for life; and, if he has to—or chooses to—he can act a role, instinctively knowing how far he can go without being hurt. All Boyle has to do is to know the outward signs and, since he is quick-witted, he can pick these up readily.

I don't mean simply that Boyle likes to act out parts; rather he knows how, chameleon-like, to find an attitude or pose that works for him at a certain moment. At one time, when he wants to condemn the clergy, he affects the Republican attitude that it was the clergy who did Parnell in; another time, when he wants to be properly middle class, he praises the clergy as the backbone of Ireland. Boyle's technique is not unlike that of 'double think' in Orwell's *1984,* except that it is more intuitive and spontaneous.

Boyle, nevertheless, is a more destructive and vulnerable figure than I have indicated. He is more destructive because he has completely failed Johnny as a father. It is not what Boyle has overtly done, but simply the fact that he obviously never cared for his family. Since Boyle was so unwilling to recognise anyone else's identity, it would be difficult for Johnny to have any self or identity of his own. Johnny could also have been so ashamed of his father that he felt driven to believe in something. He could not, however, sustain his belief, since he had no respect for authority figures who would embody the values underlying such belief. From the bitter arguments between Boyle and Johnny, particularly in Act I, it is obvious how little Johnny respects his father—and with good reason.

A comment that crystallises many of the play's implications is one Mary Boyle makes to Jerry, her former boyfriend, when he comes to console her after Bentham has deserted her and the inheritance has failed. Jerry, an earnest, ambitious young labour leader, passionately asserts that he unconditionally forgives Mary and still wants her. But when Mary remains skeptical and hints about her pregnancy, Jerry suddenly becomes unctuous and moralistic. In a flash Mary sees through him. 'Your humanity [Jerry's], is just as narrow as the humanity of the others.' She is not saying that people are inhuman, but simply how callous, opportunistic, and self-centred they have all become.

In emphasising human narrowness as a major theme, O'Casey finds that the family provides a most effective focal point. It can represent the most concrete embodiment of what full humanity can mean; conversely, the failure of humanity becomes most evident within the family situation. In Act I the Boyles exist as a family in name only as they all go their own ways, confused and self-centred. In Act II they seem united only to attain middle-class respectability and material comforts, both of which only accentuate their confusion and self-concern. Then in Act III the Boyles seem destroyed because everything turns against them. Yet precisely at this moment when Mrs. Boyle and Mary walk out on Boyle do love and responsibility become a meaningful reality. To Mary's complaint that her child will not have a father, Juno caustically replies, 'It'll have what's far better—it'll have two mothers.' But against this reality there is still Boyle, as I want to discuss him later in some detail.

To return to *The Shadow of a Gunman* again, *Juno* has the same sudden brutal contrast when fantasy gives way to reality once the inheritance becomes evident. In *Juno,* however, the suddenness seems to smack more of contrivance—or perhaps more accurately, everything seems to fall apart too conveniently. Plot-wise this is so, for O'Casey relies too much on the inheritance fiasco and Bentham's desertion of Mary to create the tragic situation he feels is inevitable. Yet, if the contrivance is too apparent, the reversal seems credible because throughout the play we see how shallow and self-centred the characters are even in their most engaging moments. Or, more accurately, they are engaging partly because they are self-centred.

If, admittedly, *Juno* does seem clumsy in plot construction in Act III, this is minor. For one thing the play has great emotional power, particularly when Mrs. Tancred expresses her grief for her son's death by praying to the

Virgin Mary to make human beings more compassionate, a prayer that Juno herself repeats after she learns that Johnny has been killed :

> ... Mother o' God, Mother o' God, have pity on the pair of us! ... O Blessed Virgin, where were you when me darlin' son was riddled with bullets, when me darlin' son was riddled with bullets! ... Sacred Heart of the Crucified Jesus, take away our hearts o' stone ... an' give us hearts o' flesh! ... Take away this murdherin' hate ... an' give us Thine own eternal love!

At the very moment the Tancreds slowly file by the Boyles' apartment to prepare for their son's funeral, the Boyles are entertaining their neighbours to impress Bentham with their affluence. Even after Mrs. Tancred's prayer, the Boyles are not deterred. Like children hungry for excitement, they rush to the window to watch the funeral procession move along, unaware of their own callousness.

What dominates the play, however, as anyone would agree, is its rich humour, which is revealed mostly in the characterisations of Juno, Boyle, Joxer Daly, and Mrs. Madigan, one of the neighbours. To speak of *Juno* is to speak of its humour, provided that we see its many ramifications. Of these four, Mrs. Madigan and Boyle stand out most.

If less prominent in the play than Juno, her neighbour Mrs. Madigan is more amusing. Like Mrs. Henderson in *The Shadow of a Gunman,* Mrs. Madigan yearns to help people, but she has all the grace of an ox. Besides, she is much less generous than Mrs. Henderson and resorts to peasant cunning when the going gets rough. After Mrs. Madigan learns that Boyle won't repay the money she lent him, she seizes a phonograph which she intends to pawn and then give the ticket to Boyle. She insists she is doing Boyle a favour because otherwise the phonograph would have been repossessed and gone for good. Mrs.

Henderson's mind would never have worked in this apparently guileless way.

Yet Mrs. Madigan's real forte is garrulous, disjointed reminiscence that she can't control and that usually back-fires. As soon as she mets Bentham, she overwhelms him with her good-natured reminiscence about Mary to ingratiate the latter with him all the more. She unconsciously combines affection and insensitivity, credulity and common sense in an astonishing *mélange* :

> An' I'm going to tell you, Mr. Bentham, you're goin' to get as nice a bit o' skirt in Mary, there, as ever you seen in your puff. Not like some of the dressed-up dolls that's knockin' about lookin' for men when it's a skelpin' they want. I remember, as well as I remember yestherday, the day she was born— of a Tuesday, the 25th o' June, in the year 1901, at thirty-three minutes past wan in the day be Foley's clock, the pub at the corner o' the street. A cowld day it was too, for the season o' the year, an' I remember sayin' to Joxer, there, who I met comin' up the stairs, that the new arrival in Boyle's ud grow up a hardy chiselur if it lived, an' that she'd be somethin' one of these days that nobody suspected, an' so signs on it, here she is to-day, goin' to be married to a young man lookin' as if he'd be fit to commensurate in any position in life it ud please God to call him !

Like Juliet's nurse, she has a vivid, if distorted, imagination in which all her life experiences are mixed up together. No wonder she embarrasses Mary beyond belief! Mrs. Madigan shows how unconsciously volatile people's feelings can be, as she takes on whatever attitude seems appropriate for the moment. While in Act II she drinks up Boyle's whiskey, in Act III she can't wait to do him in.

Less gifted in verbal infighting than Juno or Joxer, Boyle still outstrips both of them in the range and impact of his humour. Where Seumas hurts only Minnie, Boyle hurts Juno, Johnny, and Mary—though, admittedly, the play could develop this motif more. Boyle brilliantly combines apparent incongruities. Because he has no shame, he will lie outrageously and resort to illusion when necessary; yet because he overreaches himself, he is consistently exposed and outwitted. Even Mrs. Madigan brutally exposes him. He can size people up quickly and accurately and he values common sense, but when crossed he will believe whatever he chooses to and act accordingly. Underlying all these incongruities are his selfishness, his vanity that causes him never to give up, and his gay spirit. Whatever the situation, Boyle improvises a role and manipulates appearances to protect his interest; varied as these roles and appearances are, he is always 'Captain Boyle'—blowzy, cheerful, and indefatigable.

In Act I he confronts obvious but terrible difficulties. His children resent him and Juno bitterly nags him for not working, although (as suggested earlier) she may half enjoy supporting him. In this act, the most Boyle seems able to do is to keep from working and avoid a showdown with Johnny. To achieve these objectives, he plays a variety of roles in which he seems to be the butt of the humour but actually keeps himself intact. Towards Johnny he acts as the outraged parent whose authority is not being properly appreciated. Yet he doesn't want the authority because that entails responsibility. With Juno he seems to be waging a hopeless battle because he uses the most obvious tactics. He plays the sick man with pains in his legs (a role he has used many times) and that of the martyr who stoically endures the insults of a nagging wife. Yet each time Juno pounces on him and exposes him, he just shifts to another role, so that he wears her out by his persistence. When, however, circumstances change because of the news of the supposed inheritance, Boyle plays the role of the reformed sinner who vows to change his way of life. With great zeal, Boyle admits that Joxer has been his ruination.

He'll [Joxer] never blow the froth off a pint o'
mine agen, that's a sure thing. Johnny . . . Mary
. . . you're to keep yourselves to yourselves for the
future. Juno, I'm done with Joxer. . . . I'm a new
man from this out—
    (Clasping Juno's hand and singing emotionally)
O' me darlin' Juno, I will be true to thee, Me own,
me darlin' Juno. You're all the world to me.
    Curtain.

But with greater zeal he immediately becomes the faithful husband.

With Act II, Boyle plays to the hilt a somewhat
different but related role, that of the good father and
family man, the epitome of lower middle-class respectability. He reads stock reports, identifies with the parish
priest as a fellow member of the establishment, and treats
Joxer condescendingly as a faithful old retainer. In such
a role Boyle is amusing because he is so brazen; he never
hesitates a minute and always keeps his wits about him.
When Bentham impresses everyone with his fancy talk
about theosophy, only Boyle needles Bentham because he
senses that the latter is a fraud. Yet Boyle doesn't do
this too conspicuously because for the moment his own
best interests and Bentham's coincide. Even his family
help him, because they, too, worship middle-class respectability. On the other hand, Boyle foolishly tries to pass
Joxer off before Bentham as a neighbourhood celebrity,
and he shamelessly recites a sentimental poem about himself because he thinks that it is great art. If it is easy to
use appearances to indulge one's vanity, this can also be
ludicrous.

Act III brings Boyle back to the beginning, except that
his difficulties have greatly increased because the inheritance will never materialise. In place of his new suit, the
symbol of his status as the successful middle-class family
man, Boyle has put on his old moleskins; instead of
quoting the stock market, he complains again about the

pains in his legs, his old excuse for getting out of work. When Mrs. Madigan and Nugent the tailor demand their money, Boyle tries to outface them as crudely as possible. Although he succeeds with neither, he doesn't seem deterred. With the news of Mary's pregnancy, he again plays the role of the good family man, deeply concerned about his neighbourhood. Because he feels himself threatened, however, he drops the mask of affability and reveals an innate viciousness. Brazenly convinced that he is the offended party, he threatens violence if Mary doesn't leave the house. Meanwhile, to comfort himself, he goes off with Joxer to the nearest bar. Yet he also makes it clear that he needs no justification; whatever the circumstances, he can enjoy himself.

The very last episode when Boyle returns from the bar reveals how ingenious he remains despite all that he has lost, and yet how little he understands what has happened or how little he cares. Broke and blind drunk, Boyle is unaware that the bailiffs have taken away all the furniture and Juno has finally left him for good. After staggering around the apartment, he falls on a bed and imagines himself a great Irish hero:

Boyle : If th' worst comes . . . to th' worse . . . I can join a . . . flyin' column. . . . I done . . . me bit . . . in Easther week . . . had no business . . . to be . . . there . . . but Captain Boyle's Captain Boyle !

Joxer : Breathes there a man with soul . . . so . . . de . . . ad . . . this . . . me . . . o . . . wn, me nat . . . ive . . . l . . . an' !

Boyle : (*subsiding into a sitting posture on the floor*). Commandant Kelly died . . . in them . . . arms . . . Joxer. . . . Tell me Volunteer Butties . . . says he . . . that . . . I died for . . . Irelan' !

Joxer : D'jever rade Willie . . . Reilly . . . an' his
own . . . Colleen . . . Bawn? It's a darlin'
story, a darlin' story !

Boyle : I'm telling you . . . Joxer . . . th' whole
worl's . . . in a terr . . . ible state o' chassis !

From one point of view, Boyle acts ludicrously, since the
worst *has* come to the worst and he doesn't even know it.
No longer can he sponge off Juno or just use the old lies
to keep up appearances. Boyle, nevertheless, almost con-
verts this galling defeat into a victory. No matter what
happens to him outwardly, he can still believe in himself, still be gay, and uncannily adopt a pose or 'stance'
that fits the situation. But, even if Boyle may be going to
desperate lengths to nurse his vanity by identifying himself with the fallen leaders of 1916, the real impact of
his fantasy is on Juno and the ideal of Christian love and
brotherhood she expressed in her prayer to the Virgin.
For just by his drunken appearance after she leaves, he is
mocking those values which she realises the Irish desperately need to reaffirm. And since there are many more
like Boyle than like Juno, the possibility of reaffirming
this ideal in the Ireland of the play really seems more
remote. Moreover, Boyle's unconscious mockery is all the
stronger when we notice the details of his fantasy. Not
only does he imagine himself a great patriot, but when
he insists 'Commander Kelly died in these arms', he is
portraying himself as a Christian devoted to the very
ideals which Juno values but dares not claim for herself.
Boyle, however, generously portrays himself as a loving
person.

At the end of the play, then, egotism is still the
strongest force in the characters' nature and the 'state o'
chassis' endures. Although for some an alternative exists,
and for O'Casey it is the most compelling one, the
characters in the play ignore it. What is more, if Boyle's
drunken fantasy provides evidence, they all seem the

more suited to the chaos and the egotism. Consequently, *Juno* remains the most disquieting of the Dublin plays, for though what Boyle represents may be disturbing because it seems ugly, yet even in his stupor, he has considerable appeal. If he cares for no one except himself, he really takes no pains to hide it, and he is happy even when at the end he has lost all.

THE PLOUGH AND THE STARS

In *The Plough and the Stars,* the national crisis is the Easter 1916 Rising in which a few hundred Irish patriots, though outnumbered ten to one by the British, seized the Dublin General Post Office and a few other buildings and proclaimed the existence of the Irish Republic. Besides the overwhelming superiority of the British, the patriots had to confront the ignorance and indifference of the average civilian who cared more for looting than for national independence. Although the patriots fought courageously for over six days, the Rising failed dismally at the cost of heavy casualties, both military and civilian. It is true that the British virtually converted their own victory into defeat by delaying the leaders' execution. As a result, the latter became martyrs and Easter 1916 became the most important and sacred event in the Irish nationalist struggle of the twentieth century. Without denying that Easter 1916 is very important in Irish nationalism, we can also acknowledge that the Irish, particularly those who did not fight, began to romanticise the whole Rising far out of proportion to the actual event itself.[22] Even now, many years later, as the newspaper descriptions of the fiftieth celebration of the occasion revealed, Easter 1916 is very much alive for the Irish (and still a thorny subject for, as Tim Pat Coogan points out in *The World of Sean O'Casey,*[23] performances of O'Casey plays were officially discouraged during this celebration). If this was so in 1966, imagine the situation in 1926 when O'Casey wrote the play.

Therefore, just to write about Easter 1916 from the anti-heroic viewpoint of the two earlier Dublin plays makes clear what a bombshell the play could be and why it could provoke a celebrated riot in the Abbey Theatre on the fourth night of its original production.

But O'Casey does much more than this with Easter 1916. War is no longer just an ominous or disruptive, underlying force. It becomes the central reality in all the characters' lives, accentuating the suffering and waste. Furthermore, it so profoundly affects the consciousness and basic life of the country that almost for the first time it is possible to see just what are the basic forces in the nation and the people and therefore begin to confront them. Besides everything else, the war releases new energies with which the Irish must cope, for better or for worse. The foregoing are some of the reasons why I think *The Plough and the Stars* is O'Casey's masterpiece and one of the enduring great plays of the last hundred years.

The play centres on eight people of the same tenement who are all caught up in the 1916 Easter Rising, even though only one of them actually chooses to involve himself. These people represent conflicting viewpoints and aspirations which make clear both why their lives are so depressing to begin with and yet because of the war become all the worse. The Rising itself provides the structure and momentum for the action as it increasingly dominates the characters' lives. Act I, which takes place on the evening before an important patriotic rally, shows the tensions and prejudices of the Irish and some of their ridiculous feelings about war and patriotism. Act II, the night of this rally, shows the frenetic, irrational behaviour of these people as they are aroused by the passionate rhetoric of the speaker and as their own everyday frustrations and prejudices become accentuated. Act III, several months later, takes place at the height of the rebellion. It reveals the frenzy of absurd and yet genuinely heroic action, as well as terrible suffering, that took place. Act IV, which occurs a few days later, shows the Irish overwhelmingly defeated and their suffering greatly increased as the British close in and bring the rebellion to an inglorious end.

In depicting how the war takes over his characters' lives, O'Casey particularly attacks the romantic ideals serving to justify it, by showing how foolish and dangerous these can be to a people such as the Irish. In the first place, there is a stunning incongruity between these ideals and the anti-heroic character and behaviour of the Irish. The one character who chooses to fight, Jack Clitheroe, a young, ambitious, well-intentioned person with a strong desire for good middle -class respectability, does so mainly to satisfy his vanity. Clitheroe, as his neighbours caustically point out, had joined the Irish Citizens' Army because he liked wearing a splendid officer's uniform. Disgruntled because he was not promoted and influenced by his wife Nora's pleas that he remain with her, Clitheroe had become inactive. When he learns, however, that he is promoted to Commandant, he rejoins the army despite a bitter argument with his wife. Clitheroe storms off to the rally, is intoxicated by the speaker's rhetoric, and in the Rising itself is killed just before the final surrender. More foolish and petty in his patriotism is Nora's Uncle Peter, a waspish, fearful old man for whom patriotism merely consists of wearing a gaudy green uniform of the Foresters (a patriotic national organisation) and parading once a year to the grave of the eighteenth century Irish patriot Wolfe Tone. When the rebellion actually does break out, Uncle Peter quickly forgets about patriotism of any variety. Too cowardly to make the effort to loot, he adopts a high and mighty self-righteous tone towards those who do.

Not only do the Irish become patriots for the wrong reasons, but they have no sense of national purpose or identity. Instead, throughout the play the characters quarrel violently and foolishly about religion, politics, labour unions, or something as trivial as the ownership of a baby carriage. Act II provides a fine example of how divisive the Irish are at the very moment they should be united. The action takes place in a bar from which it is possible to see the silhouette of the speaker and to hear him passionately exhort his audience to act as a proud nation with a single will. But inside the bar characters contradict him by quarrelling and fighting so much that the bartender has to throw some of them out.

To add to their difficulties, the Irish simply can't deal with the problems in their everyday lives, let alone take on the burden of a war. Poverty-stricken, frustrated, and ignorant, they can do little except accentuate their misery. The terrible plight of Mollser, a consumptive young girl who doesn't have a chance to survive, forcefully illustrates the characters' general helplessness. The wretched living conditions in the tenements obviously are the primary cause, since the consumption rate in Dublin was (as indicated in the Introduction) almost the highest in Europe. But Mollser's condition is possibly aggravated by her mother's failure to give her much attention or consideration. Confused and harassed by her environment and so resigned to misery, Mrs. Gogan makes only token efforts to take care of Mollser. Under *no* circumstances could Mrs. Gogan have saved Mollser, but she might have appreciated her more, especially since Mollser is one of the few people in the tenement who can see how foolishly the Irish act in the grip of nationalist fervour.

Nor do the few people in the tenement who aspire to something nobler, either for themselves or others, fare any better. They either ridiculously oversimplify their efforts or make them self-centred and romantic. Nora's cousin, the Covey, illustrates the former. He is a young worker intellectual who is convinced that the only solution to Ireland's problem is Marxism. Unfortunately, the Covey has read just one book on the subject and does nothing but talk dogmatically and ignorantly about the revolution to everyone he meets. The last thing he would know how to do—or dare to do—is become an actual revolutionary. Behind all his big talk, he remains a mischievous, frightened boy. He spends hours tormenting

Uncle Peter, but is so scared when Rosie, the prostitute, makes up to him in the bar that in self-defence he denounces her as immoral.

Nora herself represents the person whose efforts are too narrowly selfish. Like Mary Boyle in *Juno,* Nora is intelligent and discriminating enough to want a better life. For her such a life consists of stylish clothes, a neat, artistically furnished apartment, and complete absorption in her marriage from which she can exclude the outside world. Although Nora is intelligent enough to see through Jack who masks his selfish feelings under the guise of patriotism, she can't recognise her own selfish motives. By urging Jack to sacrifice everything for their love, she also is demanding that he give up everything for her.

Not only is there such a terrible incongruity between the heroic ideals of patriotism and sacrifice and the anti-heroic everyday life of the characters, but these ideals themselves turn out to be foolish and destructive. Here Act II again serves as a fine example. In this act O'Casey conceived the brilliant and daring idea of having the silhouetted speaker present excerpts from a famous funeral oration delivered at the grave of O'Donovan Rossa by Commandant Padraic Pearse, one of the leaders of Easter 1916.[24] These are excerpts that an Irish audience would immediately recognise just as an English audience would now recall Winston Churchill's 'Blood, toil, tears, and sweat.' O'Casey goes even further, however, by leaving out some of Pearse's qualifying remarks. As William Armstrong points out,[25] O'Casey makes the speaker angrily exalt violence as a noble ideal and deny the sacred value of life :

Comrade soldiers of the Irish Volunteers and of the Citizen Army, we rejoice in this terrible war. The old heart of the earth needed to be warmed with the red wine of the battlefields. . . . Such august homage was never offered to God as this :

> the homage of millions of lives given gladly for love
> of country. And we must be ready to pour out the
> same red wine in the same glorious sacrifice, for
> without shedding of blood there is no redemption!

Since we hear Pearse's words only as they are juxtaposed
to the characters' boasting and quarrelling, these lines
become ironical because they neither fit the people nor
the situation. Moreover, these lines seem irresponsible
because they so stir up the characters that they later
become (as the stage directions tell us) 'mesmerised.' It is
risky to exhort anyone with such rhetoric; it is downright
foolhardy to do so before such an audience as that in the
bar—and by implication outside.

If reckless disregard of human life is not bad enough,
the simple fact is that the heroic ideals don't square with
the political realities of the situation. When the British
soldiers appear, they don't act like a vengeful enemy out
to destroy the Irish. They are just well-meaning,
ignorant, and prejudiced common people, who greatly
resemble the Irish, except that they are more casual and
callous. The very fact that the British can take over so
easily (except for some comments by Fluther at the end
of Act IV, the play does not emphasise their great
numerical superiority) shows how completely the rebellion has failed. This is not to mention that in the background we hear the Red Cross ambulance carrying away
the wounded, and we see Nora, crazed with grief over
the loss of Jack, acting like a helpless child.

If O'Casey did nothing more than ironically contrast
the ideals of romantic heroism underlying the Easter
1916 Rising with the actual anti-heroic behaviour of the
Irish, *The Plough and the Stars* would be a great play.
But O'Casey also brilliantly inverts these very contrasts.
Confronted with terrible suffering, the Irish common
people can act responsibly and magnanimously. What
was implicit at the end of *The Gunman* and in parts of
Acts II and III of *Juno* becomes a living reality in *The*

Plough and the Stars. Foolish, irrational, and cowardly as the Irish may be most of the time, they can act responsibly and magnanimously when they suffer terribly. At this point the Irish act as individuals involved in common suffering and are genuinely heroic. Unfortunately, the transformation occurs only at this point and at an appalling cost.

Acting as individuals and yet concerned with others they care about, the Irish can be bluntly realistic. Some of them—Nora, Mollser, Fluther, and Bessie—have tough common sense which enables them to see how foolish and reckless their neighbours can be. Nora tries hard to make Jack realise the destructive force of his vanity that causes him to rejoin the Citizens' Army after he learns of his promotion. But he is deaf to her pleas. Only consumptive Mollser can share Nora's views, as she plaintively asks Nora, after all the people of the tenement have impetuously rushed to the rally, 'Is there anybody goin', Mrs. Clitheroe, with a tither o' sense?' Coming as the last line of Act I, Mollser's comment has the force of prophetic irony.

Besides being able to expose their own folly, the Irish can accept the basic elemental self—not the romantic one—as a fundamental fact of life. For all their bravado and rhetoric, the Irish don't forget their sensual natures, as the very setting of the bar in Act II reveals. While most of the Irish misconstrue Pearse's fervent pleas or ignore them, Rosie, the prostitute who operates from the bar, and Fluther become affectionately drunk together. At the end of Act II, as Clitheroe and his comrades in their 'mesmerised' state prepare to begin a mock attack on Dublin Castle, the British governmental headquarters for Ireland, Rosie and Fluther emerge from the back of the bar gaily singing an earthy song and go off to bed together. It is true that such behaviour suggests how exaggerated and strained and to that extent false are the feelings of both the speaker and audience at the rally.

Yet it also shows that some people readily accept their natural selves.

If Act II shows us the joyous natural self, Act III shows us how terrible and ugly it can also sometimes be. Again it is Nora who passionately affirms the real nature of the Irish after she makes a wild trip through the streets at the height of the battle to try to save Jack from his folly. Not only does she fail to find him, but she is attacked by Irish women who criticise her because she dares admit that she cares more for her husband's life than for Ireland's honour. As Nora points out to Mrs. Gogan, the women are too ashamed and cowardly to admit their real desires :

> I can't help thinkin' every shot fired 'll be fired at Jack, an' every shot fired at Jack'll be fired at me. What do I care for th' others? I can think only of me own self. . . An' there's no woman gives a son or a husband to be killed—if they say it, they're lyin', lyin' against God, Nature, an' against themselves! . . .

On the other hand, while the play affirms a basic elemental self as fundamental, it also affirms an even larger fact. People can be self-less, able to involve themselves with others. One such sign is personal honesty and affirmation of common interests that transcends—or at least temporarily negates—differences. In this regard, I would particularly emphasise the very amusing episode towards the end of Act III when Bessie and Mrs. Gogan, who previously quarrelled violently over a pram they both wanted to use for looting purposes, return together, sharing the pram. As the stage directions reveal, the *'pride of a great joy illuminates their faces'*. Their loot is worthless and their taste is vulgar—not to mention that, while they have looted, other Irishmen have died in the streets. Still, as O'Casey himself has pointed out,[26] it took great courage to go out in the streets to loot. What is more, at this point Bessie and Mrs. Gogan honestly reveal their feelings and stop pretending to one another. Bessie and Mrs. Gogan now seem to be members of an authentic community that has replaced the discord and hypocrisy in much of Acts I and II. While they certainly don't become intimate friends from this point on, Mrs. Gogan in Act IV does appreciate Bessie's kindness toward Mollser, whereas previously she seemed unaware of its existence.

Another affirmation of genuine community is that of personal friendship, or tolerant understanding and concern for those one cares for. Here Fluther more than any other character acts on such a basis. Despite his arguments with the Covey about religion and labour or his peppery ridicule of Uncle Peter, Fluther consistently tries to get people to understand each others' viewpoints. Admittedly, in the bar scene in Act II, he has little, if any, success in trying to get Bessie and Mrs. Gogan to appreciate each other's frustrations. But he does try. He does, however, have real success in a more important situation. It is Fluther who, despite the very real danger, goes out in search of Nora and brings her back safe. Otherwise, considering how distraught she was, she probably would have collapsed somewhere in the streets. Nor does Fluther boast about this, in contrast to his behaviour in Act II when he tells the Covey (who is annoying Rosie) how tough he is. In the face of apparent suffering (Rosie's alleged insults from the Covey), Fluther reacts conventionally as a gallant defender of womanhood, which represents another variation on romantic idealism. In the face of real suffering, he acts courageously, provided that he values the person whose life is in danger. Just before Fluther prepares to go looting, he refuses to help a wealthy lady who has become lost during the fighting and begs him for help. In this instance, he refuses because he values looting more than he does saving the life of such a woman. He would act otherwise if Mrs. Gogan, Mollser, or Bessie were involved—though probably not Uncle Peter, whom he would ridicule as a coward.

Important as friendship qualified by self-interest may be, even more important is strong compassion for suffering humanity. In the name of Christianity, Commandant Pearse in Act II exalts violence : '. . . People in Ireland dread war because they do not know it. Ireland has not known the exhilaration of war for over a hundred years. When war comes to Ireland, she must welcome it as she would the angel of God. . . .' In ironical contrast stands the Christianity of Bessie Burgess. Although Bessie hates the Irish nationalists, she still cares for them as suffering individuals, because in the eyes of God all suffering people, regardless of their folly and hostilities, are equal and merit His love. Not only does she care for her neighbours during the Rising, but she does more to relieve their suffering than anyone else in the play. In Act III, during the heat of the battle, she takes time to get Mollser some milk, rescues Nora when she collapses in the streets after Jack angrily leaves her, and when Fluther is too drunk to move, later goes for a doctor for Mollser. In Act IV Bessie not only cares for Mollser but really becomes the central figure to whom the others instinctively turn. (Visually this is evident because Act IV takes place in Bessie's small attic apartment to which all the survivors have retreated.) And it is Bessie who sacrifices her own life when she rushes to the window and saves Nora from gunfire outside. Clearly, Bessie's Christianity seems closer to the ideal of Christ's passion than does Pearse's exaltation of violence in the name of God. This very fact dramatises the radical reversal of values which has occurred in the play.

Yet, if the Irish seem transformed by what has happened, O'Casey insists finally that this just cannot be. In 'Easter 1916' Yeats concludes that 'all is changed, changed utterly . . .'—that the Rising affirms tragic heroism as a permanent part of the Irish character and history. O'Casey, however, with heartbreaking clarity asserts that this is too simple a conclusion.

What has not changed—unless for the worse—is the persistence of the romantic ideal justifying war and personal sacrifice. After all the suffering and death, the characters still do not understand what the fighting has been about, nor do they question the value of patriotism. In a humorous vein this is evidenced by the way Fluther boasts to the English soldiers about Irish bravery. We see more pathetic consequences in the scene in which Brennan (who has escaped with his life) comes to tell Nora that Jack died a hero. Brennan, Jack, and their general all are certain that when Nora hears how bravely Jack died, she will feel happy and inspired. For Jack to imagine this after his bitter quarrel with Nora in Act III can represent only the height of folly. In reality, the case is even worse as we see in the episode itself. While Brennan rapturously describes Jack's death and his last request, Nora in her delirium appears in the doorway, completely unaware of what is going on. Even silly Uncle Peter realises how awful it would be to tell her the news about Jack.

Not only have the romantic ideals of sacrifice not changed, but the characters' efforts to change their environment are as oversimplified and precarious as ever. With a fine, ironical touch, O'Casey has the Covey try to provoke a political argument with one of the British soldiers so that he can boast about the importance of socialism. The soldier completely demolishes the Covey by agreeing with him that he too is a socialist. If the Covey were really a good revolutionary, he might have been delighted with such news. Of course he isn't. The fact that Nora has been reduced to helplessness might suggest that for her 'all is changed'. While from one point of view this is literally true (she is out of her mind), it is just as important to realise that Nora suffers so much precisely because she could not change her values and reactions during the war. Having only her vision of romantic domestic bliss, when that goes, she is much worse off than her most foolish neighbours.

Nevertheless, a great deal remains changed. It is true that Fluther, Uncle Peter, and the Covey resume playing cards and arguing, despite Nora's agony, and that Mrs. Gogan still finds her one source of pleasure in fantasising about others' funerals. But, even while playing cards, Uncle Peter, the Covey, and Fluther show how much they appreciate Bessie's kindliness and how much they care for Nora. If they are helpless to do anything, there is nothing that anyone except Bessie can do at the moment. When, however, Bessie is shot, Mrs. Gogan, who never did much for her own Mollser, immediately takes Bessie's place and begins caring for Nora. At the same time Mrs. Gogan, even more than Mrs. Grigson at the end of *The Gunman,* compassionately feels the terrible finality of Bessie's death : 'Oh, God help her, th' poor woman, she's stiffenin' out as hard as she can ! Her face has written on it th' shock o' sudden agony an' her 'ands whitenin' into th' smooth shininess of wax.'

Not only do the characters care more for one another, but they show some rudimentary self-control and self-awareness. In this regard, the most dramatic example is the great patience and restraint that Bessie shows toward Nora until the moment of her death. Such patience and restraint seem so unexpected because Bessie hated Nora for trying to escape from her slum environment. Such hatred is evident in Act I by the way Bessie brutally picks a fight with Nora for no apparent reason. In Act IV Bessie controls such feelings until she realises that she has been shot trying to save Nora. Only then does her hatred, which has been pent up, burst out, 'I've got this through . . . through you . . . through you, you bitch, you ! . . . O God have mercy on me ! . . . (*To Nora*) You wouldn't stop quiet, no, you wouldn't, blast you ! . . .'

Besides her self-control, Bessie also can be honest with herself. When she realises that no one else can come to her rescue, she begs Nora to help, and the weaker she becomes the more poignantly she pleads : 'Jesus Christ, me sight's goin'! It's all dark, dark! Nora, hold me hand!' Perhaps I am just ignoring the obvious, that in the face of death anyone would be candid and that there-fore these lines just emphasise the horror of death. But other speeches in the face of death, such as that of Lt. Langon, the fatally wounded comrade whom Jack and Brennan try to evacuate to safety from the battle, have a more self-preoccupied and fearful tone. Consequently, for Bessie to expose her weakness in such a direct and unself-conscious way reveals courage and candour.

If the Irish then act more responsibly, sensibly, and compassionately, still this has not made their lot any better. If anything, it has become worse, because they have less control over their lives. By the end of the play, just to survive the Irish have to act more effectively as individuals than they did before. Here again Bessie's death scene and its aftermath are crucial, particularly in relation to the appearance of the British soldiers, whose actions extend and complicate the implications of the play. Having the British kill Bessie, who not only sup-ports their cause but has a son fighting for them in Belgium, accentuates the folly of war. But this action has other, ironical implications. Compared with the Irish, the British soldiers as individuals are more sensible and realistic in their ideas about war. If they could help it, they certainly wouldn't shoot at civilians. But, since they have orders to shoot anyone who might seem to be a sniper —and there are snipers—they feel they have no choice. Killing Bessie is therefore an unfortunate but under-standable error.

Yet, because such an action can be understandable and logical, the war becomes more dangerous, for now it can be more easily justified. War is terrible enough when waged by the Irish as wild amateurs; yet it is perhaps more ter-rible when waged by realistic professionals who more readily disregard the individuals involved. Still it does not follow that it would have been any better for the Irish to have won the war because they might also have developed into competent professionals.

The most important consequence of all, however, is the characters' changed relationship to their environment and to historical events. In Acts I and II, while the characters certainly did not determine policies of war and peace, they did affect their outcome. The fact that Jack and his comrades were 'mesmerised' by Commandant Pearse's rhetoric and that virtually all the characters were blind to their own motives made it more probable that the uprising could be as confusing, violent, and destructive as it was. But in Act IV the most terrible irony is that, while the individual characters do act more sensibly and responsibly, they have much less control over their lives. This is particularly evident in the case of the British, the supposed victors. I say 'supposed' because the British not only are homesick in an alien country, but they may very well have to fight in a much bloodier, more senseless war in France. At the end of the play, therefore, both the English and Irish are victims in the universal community of suffering humanity.

There are many things both large and small I could emphasise that contribute to the play's comprehensive vision : the way a single word such as 'fool' acquires a richly ironical force from one episode to another; the wild, freakish humour in many episodes, such as Fluther's boast in the bar, 'I hit a man last week, Rosie, and he's fallin' yet'; the crazy excitement of many scenes, particularly the way the characters in Act II rush in and out of the bar as they are carried away by Pearse's rhetoric; or the fine contrast in moods from one act to another, particularly how the quiet restraint of Act IV (except for Bessie's death scene) comes after the wild hysteria and confusion of most of Act III. Important as all the foregoing are, I simply want to concentrate on the logical, balanced plot structure, the play's emotional power and articulateness, and its complex, varied characterisation.

Robert Hogan in *The Experiments of Sean O'Casey* illuminates the plot structure very well.[27] Hogan shows how O'Casey (as in *The Gunman* and *Juno*) uses a structure similar to Chekhov, which combines an external action dominating the lives of the various characters and separate internal action as they are involved in the same general situation. But in *The Plough and the Stars*, O'Casey develops these internal actions more harmoniously and thoroughly. While the shattering impact of the war on Jack and Nora seems immediately most noticeable, what happens to the other characters becomes almost as important. Moreover, these internal actions consistently modify one another in an apparently casual but forceful way. From time to time Mrs. Gogan and Bessie, in the bar or on the streets during the looting, keep bumping into one another. Their collisions seem accidental yet plausible because each would be drawn to the excitement and each could not but help stir the other up. It is true that Fluther and Bessie play a more decisive role than the other characters in affecting the outcome of events, but the others could have more of an impact were they less cowardly or foolish.

As for the external action, it is clearer and has a more insistent momentum than that of the two earlier plays. Again Hogan's comments illuminate. As he points out, O'Casey portrays four distinctive, organically related phases of Easter 1916.[28] In Act I, we have the intimations of conflict and very clear indications of why it could be so disastrous for characters like those in the tenements. In Act II, there is the complication because characters recklessly rush out to the streets and let themselves be caught up in the hysteria and rhetoric. In Act III, the war closes in on the characters, drawing them back from the streets in humiliating defeat. At the same time, I would add, the war liberates the characters as individuals. This enables them to act more sensibly and naturally but also heightens their confusion. In Act IV, the characters' defeat is even greater. They sit huddled in an attic room, as far from the streets as they can get, but still not far enough, for the war again closes in on them with the appearance of the British soldiers. Each act, then, is a separate unit, a particular phase in the rebellion, and yet each energises the other. Furthermore, unlike *Juno* or *The Gunman,* there are no plot contrivances or 'gimmicks'—no bombs in suitcases or fraudulent legacies—that help precipitate the catastrophe. The complex but logical interplay of the internal and external action leads forcefully and directly to the terrible climaxes in Acts III and IV.

While the range of feeling in the play varies greatly—from exultation to pathos, and from anguish to indifference—one emotion in particular dominates, that of anger. There is Bessie's vicious, unprovoked attack on Nora in Act I, Uncle Peter's tantrums whenever the Covey teases him, and Mrs. Gogan's crude but vigorous assault on Bessie in Act II, and, of course, Bessie's own assault on Mrs. Gogan, which is more provocative. Because anger dominates, it is not surprising how many kinds of argument take place. There is foolish, long-worded controversy, such as that between Fluther and the Covey in the bar, in which each proclaims that only he understands the major problems of his day, or the considerable derogatory infighting, a technique that Brennan uses with great skill. He is a crude sneerer who, when he feels himself threatened, goes for the jugular vein.

But of all the angry characters, Nora stands out as the most articulate. Nothing in the play, unless it is Bessie's final attack on Nora herself in her death scene, compares with the passionate scorn Nora heaps upon the Irish patriots and civilians she has seen in the streets during her wild search for Jack :

I tell you they're afraid to say they're afraid ! . . .
Oh, I saw it, I saw it, Mrs. Gogan. . . . At th'
barricade in North King Street I saw fear glowin'

> in all their eyes . . . An' in the middle o' th' street
> was somethin' huddled up in a horrible tangled
> heap . . . his face was jammed again th' stones, an'
> his arm was twisted around his back . . . An' every
> twist of his body was a cry against th' terrible thing
> that had happened to him. . . . An' I saw they were
> afraid to look at it. . . .

Here Nora's repetitions, her imagery with its nightmarish
clarity and intensity, and the obvious rhetorical stress in
her sentences vividly project anger bordering on frenzy.

Yet, granted the emotional power of the play, a still
more impressive feature is the characterisation, which, I
think, represents the play's greatest achievement. To say
this is not to deny the virtues of Juno and Boyle, but
only to recognise that in *The Plough and the Stars*
O'Casey is doing something different. If no one in *The
Plough and the Stars* towers over the others as Juno and
Boyle do in the earlier play, more characters are well
developed. Nora, Bessie, Fluther, and Mrs. Gogan are all
major characters, and Jack, Uncle Peter, and the Covey
also play prominent roles. This greater attention to more
characters also correlates with a greater personal
intimacy and awareness of one another which all the
characters have. In all three Dublin plays, characters
live on top of one another and are garrulously friendly
or hostile, but in *The Plough and the Stars* they have
to interact more because they live under greater tension
and need each other more, whether as targets for abuse
or as comrades to care for.

Besides the more balanced characterisation and greater
interplay, we find much greater suffering. Certainly the
intimacy I have just mentioned contributes, for what
affects one character almost has to affect the others. But
the characters suffer because they have fewer defences
and stronger feelings. If no one in this play matches
Boyle or Seumas in insulating himself against reality,
conversely no one in the earlier plays expresses the sus-

tained indignation of Nora or the plaintive helplessness of Bessie when she realises her utter loneliness as death approaches.

To the other traits I have emphasised, I would add complexity in personality and behaviour. I don't mean that O'Casey's characters in this respect compare to Chekhov's, but, except for Boyle, they certainly have more complicated reactions than those in the other plays, and the differences between men and women are much less pervasive and consistent. The men in *The Plough and the Stars* are not as boastful, vicious, and hypocritical as they are in the earlier plays; the women seem less passive and abject, and more of them share Mary Boyle's desire for a better life, even if they do nothing about it. Still another indication of the greater complexity of the characters is the way their confusion manifests itself. While the characters in the two earlier plays certainly deceive themselves and combine contradictory traits, those in *The Plough and the Stars* do so more quixotically and yet more rigorously. They seem more unpredictable and malleable, but they also can be more intense and serious.

So far as individual characters are concerned, I would for various reasons particularly emphasise three : Nora, Mrs. Gogan, and Fluther. If I am omitting Bessie, it is not because I don't think she is one of the play's most fully realised characters, but only because in other contexts I have already discussed her at considerable length.

Nora represents an interesting development of the passionate, romantic idealist trying to express her yearning for a better life. Just the strength of this yearning is itself an important reason for singling out Nora. Yet O'Casey also portrays her more critically and probingly than he does her counterparts, Minnie in *The Gunman* and Mary Boyle in *Juno,* by emphasising incongruities in her character. Certainly one obvious incongruity is that of strength and weakness or independence and dependence. Nora (as I have noted) runs her household very efficiently, orders Uncle Peter, the Covey, and Jack around, and unhesitatingly imposes her ideal upon all of them. Yet she seems virtually helpless when Bessie browbeats her and threatens to hit her. In Act III the contrast stands out more sharply. Nora risks her life to save Jack and defies all the other women whose conventional ideas of patriotic wifely behaviour she ridicules. Shortly afterwards Nora, however, becomes so helpless she has to turn to Mrs. Gogan and let the latter help her inside. Still later in Act III Nora boldly confronts Brennan and ridicules his 'patriotic' behaviour. When Jack leaves her, nevertheless, she falls prostrate to the ground, this time to be carried inside by Bessie.

More striking and significant is the incongruity between sharp objectivity and uncritical subjectivity. Here I am referring to the way Nora uses her own intelligence deceptively. While she sees through other women's defences and rationalisations, she also uses this intelligence to excuse, if not exalt, her own selfish motives. Nora fails to realise how deeply her pride and vanity are involved in her love for Jack so that a threat to Jack becomes a threat to her most exalted ego ideals. In begging Jack to stay with her as she does in Acts I and III, Nora not only acts possessively but refuses to accept him on his own terms, granted their limitations. Despite all the sympathy we feel for Nora in her anguish, we also see her own considerable responsibility for her collapse.

Mrs. Gogan, as I have mentioned, represents the relatively ignorant Catholic of decent basic instincts who lets some of her religious ideas foolishly dominate her life. She is a fatalist who believes that there is little an individual can do to control her life, and she regards death as a more significant reality than life. While these two attitudes enable some people to confront the limitations of their wretched lives tragically, for Mrs. Gogan they just provide convenient escapes.

Her fatalism manifests itself as a stylised series of

reactions to Mollser's illness in which Mrs. Gogan acts as the solicitious mother. By such reactions, Mrs. Gogan fancies herself an important actress in a drama. Without her performances as the solicitous mother, the drama is not possible; with it, she feels she has done all she can. In reality, Mollser herself is assuming the responsibility, her mother just concerns herself with her own histrionic reactions. Such histrionic reactions also help explain Mrs. Gogan's amusing fantasies about death. In these the religious idea of looking upon death as the supreme end expresses itself again in dramatic terms as a performance. When Fluther (mild hypochondriac that he is) begins worrying about his health, Mrs. Gogan pulls out all the stops as she tells him how she fears for his life :

> I dunno; there's many a man this minute lowerin' a pint, thinkin' of a woman, or pickin' out a winner, or doin' work as you're doin' while th' hearse dhrawn by th' horses with the black plumes is dhrivin' up to his own hall door, an' a voice that he doesn't hear is muttherin' in his ear, 'Earth to earth, an' ashes t'ashes, an' dust to dust.'

Then when Fluther begins sweating and says that such talk is too frightening, Mrs. Gogan replies :

> It is an' it isn't; it's both bad an' good. . . . It always gives meself a kind o' threspassin' joy to feel meeself movin' along in a mourning coach, an' me thinkin' that, maybe, th' next funeral 'll be me own, an' glad, in a quiet way that this is somebody else's.

In these two speeches Mrs. Gogan transforms the religious idea of death as the ultimate reality into a vivid, dramatic creation in which she is the star, director, and audience.

Besides escaping histrionically from her ugly life, Mrs. Gogan does so by running down her neighbours, a sport in which almost all the characters participate. None, however, display her talent. When she sees Uncle Peter,

putting on his uniform for the parade, she remarks to
Fluther :

> Isn't oul' Peter a funny-lookin' little man? . . . Like
> somethin' you'd pick off a Christmas Tree . . . When
> he's dhressed up in his canonicals, you'd wonder
> where he's been got. God forgive me, when I see him
> in them, I always think he must ha' had a Mormon
> for a father! He an' th' Covey can't abide each
> other; the pair o' them is always at it, thryin' to best
> each other. There'll be blood dhrawn one o' these
> days.

Like Maisie Madigan in *Juno*, Mrs. Gogan has great
vigour, a sure pictorial sense, and an astonishing array of
prejudices to draw upon. Mrs. Gogan has no idea why
she acts as she does and has only the foggiest notion of
what national events mean. She, nevertheless, has pro-
digious energy that she expends wastefully but also half
originally. In a bumbling way, her basically kind feelings
come out only when she directly confronts suffering and
the romantic facades she has constructed collapse.

For Fluther, too, incongruity plays an important role
in his character. After all, Fluther is a boaster and fool
like Captain Boyle in *Juno* and yet an authentic hero
who can be courageous, concerned about others, accepting (both of himself and others), and realistic. In contrast to Nora, incongruity in Fluther reveals itself in a
more amusing and engaging way.

Fluther, in being courageous and concerned for others,
is quixotic in his reactions. He minimises the really significant things but calls attention to the minor ones,
though without being hypocritical. He never mentions
that he risked his life to rescue Nora, but he proudly
shows Nora in Act I how good a job he did in putting a
new lock on her door. In his tolerance Fluther displays a
fine sense of proportion. Not even the Covey, for
example, ridicules Uncle Peter the way Fluther sometimes does. Fluther does so only when this is absolutely

necessary for Uncle Peter's own good; the Covey, whenever he wishes to be irrascible. Conversely, when Mrs.
Gogan excessively and unfairly criticises Nora Fluther
defends her without alienating Mrs. Gogan. In Act II,
while virtually everyone attacks Bessie for being so vicious
in the bar, Fluther openly pleads with them to try to
understand the strain under which Bessie labours because
her son is at war. In both episodes Fluther judges people
by their own merits and yet tries to accommodate himself
to their feelings.

Besides his concern and tolerance, Fluther has a real
talent for letting himself go. He not only accepts his
sensual impulses but dramatises and unabashedly enjoys
them. At the end of Act III while everyone else loots
clothing and food, Fluther takes only whiskey; and while
people are dying in the streets, Fluther reels in singing
exultantly :

> Fluther's a jolly good fella! . . . Fluther's a jolly
> good fella!
> Up the rebels! . . . That nobody can deny! (*He
> beats on the door*) Get us a mug or a jug, or some-
> thin', some o' yous, one o' yous, will yous, before I
> lay one o' yous, out! . . . (*Looking down the street*)
> Bang an' fire away for all Fluther cares. . . . (*Bang-
> ing at door*) Come down, an' open th' door, some o'
> yous, one o' yous, will yous, before I lay some o' yous
> out! . . . Th' whole city can topple home to hell, for
> Fluther!

More arresting but foolish is the image Fluther projects of himself as a ladies man and a good Irishman—
a courageous, powerful, resourceful, and destructive
figure, a killer with his fists. This is the Fluther who
'rescues' Rosie from the Covey's insults by challenging
him to a fight. Here Fluther is a comic figure because he
blusters so energetically without landing a blow or daring
to, and because he tells such outrageous lies about his
strength. In this episode the bartender really prevents a

fight by throwing out the Covey, since the latter isn't really as good a customer as Fluther. But Fluther claims a great victory and sees himself as a superior man. 'I wasn't goin' to let meself be malignified by a chancer . . . He got a little too derogatory for Fluther . . . Be God, to think of a cur like that comin' to talk to a man like me.'

The very comprehensiveness of the play's vision, particularly its enormous range of contrasts, produces two markedly different impressions, which together crystallise the impact and significance of the play. Such contrasts so expand our awareness of contradiction, argument and frustration in human life that they could make almost any situation, even nuclear holocaust, conceivable, and human survival credible and moving. In this regard the very last episode, the return of the British soldiers to Bessie's apartment, after they have herded the male survivors off to a church for temporary detention, is a good example. Finding the apartment deserted, except for Bessie's body lying covered on the floor, and having nothing more they can do until the very last remnants of the Irish are defeated, the British sit down and drink some tea. From one point of view, such behaviour seems unusually callous, since the British themselves have just killed Bessie, their own ardent supporter in the area. On the other hand, the British have already expressed their regrets for shooting Bessie, they are far from home, and more helpless than the Irish. And the fact that they can for just a moment put aside the war indicates that they are sensible and resilient, not governed by rigid absolutes.

Such an episode forcefully reminds us that human beings have an extraordinary capacity to accommodate themselves to situations over which they have no control. But such accommodation can create terrible burdens and intolerable frustrations for someone as idealistic and romantic as the O'Casey I described in the Introduction. A man who loved beauty and for whom education had such creative possibilities, who had a compelling vision of social revolution and a militant Christian faith, who recognised in so many of the people in his environment courage, vitality, and an overwhelmingly yearning for a better life—such a man could hardly settle for accommodation, regardless of how admirable and impressive it may be.

It is therefore not surprising that O'Casey should try to change some of the implications of the great tragicomic vision of *The Plough and the Stars*; more specifically to see if it is possible to assert more control over the forces affecting one's life and to try to fulfill one's deepest yearnings, by redirecting many of the energies he legitimately valued so much in the Dublin poor. And this is precisely what O'Casey tries to do in all his succeeding plays. Yet to do so is not easy because the comprehensiveness and precision of the vision means that changes themselves must be commensurate with the rest of the vision to make their impact evident. At the same time, given such a large vision, it isn't easy to deal with smaller, more casual subjects, because the incentive remains to make them part of the entire vision, even though they may have a separate existence of their own.

In short, *The Plough and the Stars* is a great achievement, but one that casts a shadow over the rest of O'Casey's work.

TOWARDS A NEW JERUSALEM

The Silver Tassie	1929
	Published 1928
Within the Gates	1934
	Published 1933
Purple Dust	1944
	Published 1940
The Star Turns Red	1940
Red Roses for Me	1943
	Published 1942
Oak Leaves and Lavender	Published 1946

Although O'Casey in his autobiographies devotes much less attention to his life in England than he does to that in Ireland, still we can piece together some details concerning the years 1926–1946, which roughly constitute this middle or 'heroic' phase of O'Casey's dramatic career.

The keen interest in political and social life persists (as I noted in the Introduction), though not as strong as it was in his earlier life. O'Casey seems to be more of an observer or commentator than a participant. For example, he recounts at considerable length a meeting with Stanley Baldwin, the most important and powerful Tory Prime Minister between the two World Wars. While Baldwin expressed the standard views that the British ruling class held of the Irish, O'Casey in contrast seemed to understand British politics fairly well.[29] In fact, he understood these politics so well that he had a great time playing the innocent with Baldwin! The latter, because of his standard prejudice simply took everything O'Casey said literally. As a result, Baldwin brilliantly demonstrated just how obtuse the English ruling class can be (a theme that turns up in *Purple Dust*).

Another impression we get is that O'Casey enjoyed (at least for a few years) some literary renown. He describes interviews with journalists and meetings with some of the English literary establishment. It is true that O'Casey adopts a facetious tone and ridicules the journalists and the literary lions. Yet he obviously appreciates the attention, particularly since it contrasted noticeably to the condescending treatment he felt he received at the hands of the Irish literary establishment and which was one of the reasons why he felt frustrated in Ireland. Unfortunately for O'Casey, such recognition did not last, for one of the consequences of the rejection of *The Silver Tassie* by the Abbey Theatre, though it did bring O'Casey considerable publicity for a while, was to hurt him at the box office. Except for a fairly popular American production of *Within the Gates* (1935) and revivals of the Dublin plays, O'Casey did not enjoy much financial success. *The Tassie* ran for two months. The London production of *Within the Gates* netted him about five pounds; *The Star Turns Red* and *Oak Leaves and Lavender* were put on at what would be at best the equivalent of off Broadway; *Red Roses for Me,* however, ran for four months; but *Purple Dust* did not receive an English production during this period.

Obviously, no playwright likes to be without a theatre, and O'Casey was no exception, especially since he was a sensitive person. What impact did this decline in popularity have on O'Casey's work? The usual explanation is that he lost his theatrical touch—or at least lost much of it—and wrote clumsy, un-theatrical plays. But at least two reasons exist why I would question the explanation. The first, as my discussion of these later plays will reveal, is that O'Casey, if anything, became more daringly theatrical. The second is that as O'Casey kept revising (as suggested in the Preface) he would enhance the plays' theatrical and dramatic potentialities. Early versions of these plays beginning with *The Silver Tassie* would reveal the basic theme of the plays, but without a very strong organising principle to create tension and shape.

In addition, individual scenes would be long and discursive, and contrasts between scenes would be muted. Early drafts of *The Silver Tassie,* for example, seemed like review sketches without much momentum; in addition, some of the incidents in Act III (which in the stage version is short) seemed long and anti-climactic.

Still another complicating factor is the assumption that if the Abbey Theatre had accepted *The Silver Tassie*

O'Casey would have had a theatre. But this assumption remains open to considerable doubt. For one thing, the Irish government had some control over the selection of plays by the Abbey, since one condition of its subsidisation of the Abbey was the right to appoint one director. Moreover, since O'Casey's plays in his exile were just as critical of the Irish, though in different respects, than the Dublin plays, it is highly doubtful that these plays would have been accepted, *The Silver Tassie* rejection notwithstanding.

While O'Casey does not mention his private life to any extent, some impressions do emerge, particularly concerning his marriage in 1928 to the Irish actress Eileen Carey. The young, beautiful affection and candour with which he writes about even their financial struggles suggests that he was very happy. Perhaps one reason why O'Casey's later plays do concern themselves with the possibility of a good life is that O'Casey himself knew the value of such a life. At the same time, as a married man with a family, O'Casey had a difficult time during these years. For example, in his autobiographies he describes how he and his wife at one point lived in a very small cottage with quite primitive facilities.[30]

During the twenty years that this second period covers, O'Casey wrote six full-length and several one-act plays (which are discussed separately in the Appendix). Although these plays all rely considerably on nonrealistic elements, they do vary considerably in form and in tone. *Purple Dust,* for example, is more light hearted than the others. Nevertheless, in all these plays (except possibly the last, *Oak Leaves and Lavender*) there is, as suggested in the Introduction, a dominant character whom we can call heroic. I would call him heroic because he embodies the aspirations and energies of the people around him but at a deeper level of thought and feeling. Moreover, he has, or is groping towards, a vision of a better, richer life. Roughly, this vision seems at one pole to be political and social, and at the other aesthetic and religious, as well as to represent varying combinations of all these. While the plays do share these common concerns, nevertheless, this does not mean that they form some architectonic whole or that it wouldn't be possible to discuss them from other points of view.

THE SILVER TASSIE

In this play O'Casey portrays the shattering impact of
World War I on Harry Heegan, a vital, exuberant Irish
athlete, and on his family and friends whose lives are
closely identified with his. In exploring this subject,
O'Casey also introduces into the play, particularly in Act
II (which takes place on a battlefield) a number of non-
realistic elements, usually called expressionistic. These
include anonymous characters, choral chants, considerable visual distortion, and contrasts in the levels of
consciousness of different characters.

Nothing that I have mentioned so far seems shocking
or outlandish. Yet, this is the play that has provoked
fierce controversy because of its rejection by the Abbey
Theatre, O'Casey's refusal to send any other plays to the
Abbey, and the possible impact of the rejection upon
O'Casey's subsequent career.[31] For such reasons, it would
seem an almost hopeless task to write about the play.
But, since most of the controversy took place forty years
ago, it just might be possible to start fresh from the play
itself. In this respect we are quite fortunate because in
London in 1969, after a forty year interval, David Jones
of the Royal Shakespeare Company directed an interesting and impressive revival.[32]

Granted that the rehearsals are not the same as the
finished production, still they do reveal a lot about the
play. For The Silver Tassie when seen, even just in
rehearsals (as I was able to),[33] turns out to be clearer,
simpler, yet richer in texture than I, for one, previously
thought. It is a wry, beautiful, and painful play in which
something so simple as Harry's injury has many ramifications, but ultimately remains just one man's agony, however much we may wish it otherwise.

The play consists of four acts, all sharply contrasting to each other, three of them centring on Harry, and one (Act II) in which he does not even appear. Act I, which takes place just before Harry is to return to the front from leave, shows him in his prime as a vital charismatic figure through whom the others live vicariously. The climax of the act comes when Harry, and his admiring friends and family, celebate a great football victory (for which he was largely responsible). In stunning contrast is Act II which takes place on a battlefield. Through the use of some of the expressionistic elements mentioned, in addition to some we could now call Pop Art, O'Casey presents a group of typical (most of them anonymous) soldiers, as they endure an ordinary day's existence at the front. While Harry (as I have said) does not appear in this act, the implication is that what happens to the rest affects him. Act III involves another forceful contrast, as we see Harry (after the war) in a hospital convalescing from a crippling spinal injury. To accentuate the contrast within the act, Harry's father and his good friend Simon Norton are also patients. (In Ireland it was not uncommon for civilians, even with minor ailments, to be hospitalised in the same wards along with seriously wounded World War I veterans.) Harry is embittered because of what he has had to give up and because his family and friends neither understand nor help him. They, in turn, are confused and embarrassed because they can't endure seeing him and don't know how to respond. Act IV shifts to an entirely different setting, a banquet of Harry's old team to which he has been invited for old times sake. The banquet, however, only accentuates the alienation between Harry and his family, particularly when Harry loses his girl to his best friend and war comrade. All Harry can do is try to establish a new life for himself, whatever its nature may be. Meanwhile, his family and friends smugly continue their lives which are more fortunate than his but still drab.

Certainly the most immediate impact of *The Tassie*

is an attack on the inhumanity of war. This theme reveals itself in minor details. We see a group of soldiers worn out from fatigue duty, callous civilian officials out to inspect conditions at the front, and stretcher bearers removing the wounded. But the basic details of the setting and action reveal the inhumanity more forcefully. Dominating the scene is a cannon, on which lies a figure called the Croucher (a soldier driven mad by the war). The Croucher serves as a choral commentator on the action by issuing a thundering prophecy from Ezekiel in which he describes the whole setting as a valley of bones.

In the background is a ruined monastery from which occasionally come voices singing parts of the mass. At the same time, the soldiers moving in front of the ruined monastery also chant many of their verse complaints to the liturgy of the mass. Through these juxtapositions and ironical reversals, O'Casey emphasises that war denies the most fundamental value of Christianity, the sacredness of human life. Not without reason did historians call this the Great War because casualties on both sides greatly exceeded those on the Western Front in World War II. At the Battle of the Somme alone, British casualties were 410,000.[34] Moreover, both sides kept trying continually to overwhelm the other by attempting periodic break-throughs. Even defensive strategy was suicidal for, regardless of the cost, units could not abandon a position.

After such casualty figures, to mention the physical conditions seems trifling, but the rain really did seem almost unending, so that the soldiers' complaint about the rain was relevant, just as was another detail, that in which Harry's comrade, Barney, for some reason the only soldier mentioned by name in the act, stands throughout the entire act tied to a gun wheel as punishment for stealing a chicken. We might think this a ludicrous exaggeration, but, as the historian Cruttwell points out,[35] British military justice was so severe that it shocked some of the Germans.

Yet O'Casey is doing much more than attacking war.

His real originality results from his emphasis on—I should even say his celebration of—the soldiers' strong and subtle instincts for survival. Although the soldiers express their weariness and disgust, they don't indulge in self-pity. Instead they are lively and humorous. They think nostalgically of home, but they never forget their immediate needs. And even their memories of civilian life often are moving, particularly when sung by actors with good voices (as was true of the 1969 London revival).

> Would God I smok'd an' walk'd and watch'd th'
> Dance of a golden Brimstone butterfly
> To the saucy pipe of a greenfinch resting
> In a drowsy, brambled lane in Cumberland.

As the pressure mounts, two other conflicting impulses begin expressing themselves in the men. The first is a yearning for a richer, more meaningful life that has some spiritual values; the second is the men's bitter awareness that self preservation is their most compelling need. When the soldiers learn that a break-through may be imminent, they rush to load their cannon! At the same time, they sing a hymn which expresses this grim awareness of their dilemma:

> Corporal: (*singing*): Hail, cool-hardened tower of
> steel emboss'd
> With the fever'd, figment thoughts of man;
> Guardian of our love and hate and fear,
> Speak for us to the inner ear of God!
>
> Soldiers: We believe in God and we believe in thee.

In building up Act II to this climax, O'Casey certainly emphasises the men's tragic plight. But just as noticeable is their bold criticism of the war and their dignity in the face of danger. Consequently, though the men accept violence to preserve their own lives, they themselves *do not act* violently. While they have no defence against death, they can decide how they will confront it. And to them such a decision is important, for it means that they are not abrogating their responsibility, but actually extending it.

Yet, unlike *The Plough and the Stars*, *The Silver Tassie* is not just a war play. We could even argue that the war simply brings into the sharpest focus the problems and issues that Act I introduces. For what Act I makes clear is the tremendous power of the life force which affects everyone in varying degrees, but which Harry most strongly embodies. In fact, he worships it, though no one, not even Harry himself, understands this at the time.

Throughout most of Act I, it is obvious how strongly Harry affects those around him. His father, Sylvester, and the latter's good friend, Simon Norton, derive their supreme pleasure from recounting Harry's triumphs and vicariously experiencing them; Susie Monican, a neighbour, waiting to go off to war to be a nurse, has become so angry and frustrated that Harry hasn't responded to her sexually that she has sublimated her desire into a fierce religiosity that Simon and Sylvester call 'tambourine theology'. And although none of the others realise it, Harry embodies for them those basic energies which they consider most important for living. They are identifying with him but without understanding the implications. (This helps explain why, when Harry is injured, they are so inarticulate.)

When Harry does return, fresh from his victory, we can see clearly just how and why he affects people so strongly. He is direct and unashamed of his responses. Just as important, he is articulate. It is not enough that he has enjoyed his triumph, he wants everyone to share it with him.

> Slipping by the back rushing at me like a mad bull, steadying a moment for a drive, seeing in a flash the goalie's hands sent with a shock to his

chest by the force of the shot, his half-stunned
motion to clear, a charge, and then carrying him, the
ball and all with a rush into th centre of the net!

He is so excited that he would even risk going AWOL,
just to show his recklessness. When all the others dissuade
him, he still insists upon a victory toast so as not to waste
a single moment of joy.

Not only is Harry more vital than the others, but he
believes so passionately in a life of joy that he almost
apotheosises it. The others, however, have a much
narrower conception of its value. Harry's neighbour,
Mrs. Foran, simply has a vague notion that when her
husband returns to the front she will be gay. It never
dawns on her that by expressing her joy while her husband is home on leave, she is hurting him. For Harry's
mother, the joy of life scarcely exists. Worn out, sickly,
and embittered by a difficult life, all she can visualise are
narrow self interest and petty detail. To her Harry's survival seems less important than his dependency allow-
ance, which his girl friend, Jessie, almost received.

To see Harry leave for the front so exultant and then
to see him (at the beginning of Act III) as a helpless
cripple is almost unbearable. Even though O'Casey keeps
Harry out of sight during most of the act, his presence
dominates the hospital, especially since none of the
others can bring themselves to talk to him, except to
utter platitudes. While his family and friends realise that
they aren't helping Harry, they simply don't understand
how much his whole identity depends upon physical
vigour and joy. By trying to minimise what has happened
to him, they are denying the reality of his feelings.

An even more disturbing development in Act III is
that Jessie simply can't stand seeing Harry. To her
Harry represents all those animal instincts she wants to
express but can do so only if she is around the most
magnetic or vital male. It is she who needs Harry most
of all—but Harry as he was, which ironically means, at

present, that she turns to his comrade, Barney, who has survived with only a minor wound.

Jessie aside, Harry also has his own nature to contend with. Proud, sensitive, and demanding, Harry feels conflicting emotions. His pride tells him that he has lost Jessie and his youth; self-pity makes him feel that this should never have happened to him of all people.

In Act IV, even though people pay more attention to Harry and have begun to try to find ways to help him, they only make matters worse. He becomes more aware of what he is missing and less able to control his feelings, especially as he watches Barney and Jessie dancing. In the meantime, the others either uncomfortably ignore him or again try to humour him by encouraging him to do his best when it comes to his turn to contribute to the evening's entertainment by playing his ukulele. (This is his great achievement now!)

Unable to control his desire and his rage, Harry keeps following Barney and Jessie around, hoping to find them alone making love. Upon discovering them, he denounces Jessie as a whore. When she denies the charge, Harry only becomes angrier and more cruel. Barney, who until this moment has tried to be patient, now feels insulted and savagely attacks Harry. Only Jessie's screams and Surgeon Maxwell's appearance save Harry. Certainly at this point Harry is humiliated and helpless, all the more so when his mother and father have to take him home. On the other hand, the humiliation helps dissipate much of Harry's bitterness. Before this scene with Jessie and Barney, he couldn't confront his deepest feelings. But, at least after this scene, he experiences some relief, even if his pain may be just as great. It is ironic that in his helplessness, Harry acts more heroically than he did when he was a football great. Emphasising the disparity betweeen Harry and the others who simply go on leading their grubby little lives, might suggest a kind of final triumph for Harry. But this is not so at all.

Like *Juno and the Paycock*, the play does not end at

this point, for O'Casey explores more ironies in this situation. After Teddy and Harry leave, Jessie for a moment feels sorry for Harry. But Susie points out to her that no one can possibly help Teddy and Harry and that the healthy are entitled to their lives :

> Oh nonsense ! If you'd passed as many through your hands as I, you'd hardly notice one. (*To Jessie*) Jessie, Teddy Foran and Harry Heegan have gone to live their own way in another world. Neither I nor you can lift them out of it. No longer can they do the things we do. We can't give sight to the blind or make the lame walk. We would if we could. It is the misfortune of war. As long as wars are waged, we shall be vexed by woe; strong legs shall be made useless and bright eyes made dark. But we, who have come through the fire unharmed, must go on living. (*Pulling Jessie from the chair*) Come along and take your part in life ! (*To Barney*) Come along, Barney, and take your partner into the dance !

Then to make her point more emphatic, Susie dances away with Surgeon Maxwell who is singing a song that ironically reverses lines which Harry himself uttered just a few moments earlier ! 'For he is a life on the ebb / We a full life on the flow.'

Susie is right in pointing out that the healthy can't perform miracles, that what has happened to Harry may have been unfair but was a fact of life, and that those who have vitality should enjoy it. Nor is she claiming that God has saved her or that by her actions she will benefit humanity.

And when we look back at the others in the play, can we blame them for what happened to Harry? And has anyone enjoyed watching him suffer? Or could anyone as vital as Jessie possibly have been happy with Harry or made him happy? Moreover, in the confrontation between Barney and Harry, Jessie tried to be fair to both. The cruel truth which Susie is acknowledging is that injustice is part of the human condition and life is so valuable and uncertain that those who can enjoy it should do so if they can.

But Susie's comments don't represent the last word either, for her tone is important, as well as the timing of Surgeon Maxwell's song. For her tone is both callous and sanctimonious, and Maxwell's song uncomfortably arrogant. Neither the comment, the song, nor Mrs. Foran's curtain line speech which reduces Harry to a child will change things:

It's a terrible pity Harry was too weak to stay an' sing his song, for there's nothing I love more than the ukulele's tinkle, tinkle in the night-time.

Still, there would be less pain, if at least the healthier people were not so hard. Yet it is this hardness, not really cruelty, not even selfishness, which crystallises for O'Casey just what the war has done or released in human beings who have survived.

As such survivors, Simon and Sylvester play an interesting role. To a certain extent, they remind us of Boyle and Joxer because they are idle, detached, and boastful. But they differ considerably from Joxer and Boyle because, though no more cunning, they are more intelligent and more generous in their judgments.

We are most aware of Harry's and Teddy's helplessness in the hospital scene in Act III in contrast to Simon and Sylvester. While the latter act as children unwilling to take a bath or afraid of an operation, Harry and Teddy have to struggle hard to try simple things, only to discover that they can't do them. In reading the play, we might feel that Sylvester's and Simon's antics and their obvious ineffectuality seem overdone because by comparison they diminish the stature of whatever Harry and Teddy do. But, as we see in production, while Simon and Sylvester can't even take a bath, it doesn't matter. They are still healthy, and can even cultivate their petty ailments. Such a reverse comparison makes us realise all the more that Teddy and Harry are really helpless people. Such a comparison may also seem cruel, but I'm not certain, because Simon and Sylvester actually represent a threat to no one. Besides, they have a great talent for anatomising others' behaviour. Susie can never understand herself as well as they understand her. By their comments they almost immortalise her. At the beginning of Act III, Simon and Sylvester wryly appreciate how the war has enabled Susie to enjoy her sexuality and yet still practise her 'tambourine theology'.

Sylvester (after a pause): Be God, isn't it a good one?

Simon: Almost, almost, mind you, Sylvester, incomprehensible.

Sylvester: To come here and find Susie Monican fashion'd like a Queen of Sheba. God moves in a mysterious way, Simon.

Simon: There's Surgeon Maxwell prancing after her now.

Sylvester (stretching to see): Heads together, eh? Be God, he's kissing her behind the trees! Oh, Susannah, Susannah, how are the mighty fallen, and the weapons of war perished!

While there are a number of features of *The Tassie* that I could single out, I want to concentrate on just two. These are a particular use of contrast that shows different levels of consciousness in reaction, and some of the verses in Act II.

One of the things we are inclined to forget in emphasising O'Casey's experiments in Act II is that he also uses non-realistic elements throughout the rest of the play. (In one of the earlier drafts of the play he emphasises this in marginal comments.) There are passages, such as Simon's and Sylvester's reminiscence of Harry's great moments, that are written in a deliberately ornate prose, or Susie's religious exhortations that almost parody fundamentalist preaching! As Simon and Sylvester, while awaiting Harry's arrival from his football match, reminisce about her exploits, Susie stands near them polishing a steel helmet and denouncing them in a gaudy Biblical rhetoric :

> —Oh if the two of you only knew what it was to live ! Not to live leg-staggering an' belly-creeping among the pain-rotted and sin-splashed desires of the flesh; but to live, oh, to live swift-flying from a holy peace to a holy strength, and from holy strength to a holy joy, like the flashing flights of a swallow in the deep beauty of a summer sky.

While neither speech is expressionistic, both in striking contrast to other passages depend upon a deliberate heightening of consciousness.

Besides, there are contrasts between those who have ? and those who don't. For example, in Act III er s trying to urge Harry to wheel himself out among es and beeches on the hospital grounds. Although ans well, she is fatuous and insensitive :

> *(switching off the two hanging lights, so that the red light over the fireplace alone remains).* Don't be foolish, Twenty-eight. Wheeling your-self about among the beeches and the pines when the daffodils are hanging out their blossoms, you'll deepen your chance in the courage and renewal of the country.

Precisely because Susie's answer is so pat, Harry ridicules her by articulating this sombre vision :

> *Harry (with intense bitterness)* I'll say to the pine, 'Give me the grace and beauty of the beech'; I'll say to the beech, 'Give me the strength and stature of the pine'. In a net I'll catch butterflies in bunches; twist and mangle them between my fingers and fix them wriggling on to mercy's banner. I'll make my chair a Jug-

gernaut, and wheel it over the neck and spine
of every daffodil that looks at me, and strew
them dead to manifest the mercy of God and
the justice of man!

Susie (shocked). Shush, Harry, Harry!

While these two speeches do not differ as much as others
which juxtapose Biblical phrases with everyday speech,
still the tone and style of both speeches seem more fantastic than those of comparable speeches in the Dublin
plays.

Besides these different contrasts, I want to point out
how skilfully O'Casey in Act II uses verses that in reading seem mediocre or even silly. Yet in production such
verses become delicate and subtle. As the stretcher
bearers slowly carry the wounded to a collection statio
they chant these verses which remind us of Moth
Goose or early Blake:

1st Bearers (chanting):
　Oh, bear it gently, carry it soft—
　A bullet or a shell said stop, stop, stop.
　It's had its day, and it's left the play.
　Since it gamboll'd over the top, top, top.
　It's had its day, and it's left the play,
　Since it gamboll'd over the top.

2nd Bearers (chanting):
　Oh, carry it softly, bear it gently—
　The beggar has seen it through, through, through.
　If it 'adn't been 'im, if it 'adn't been 'im,
　It might 'ave been me or you, you, you.
　If it 'adn't been 'im, if it 'adn't been 'im,
　It might 'ave been me or you.

The stretcher bearers are urging that we treat the
wounded as gently as people treat animals they love. The
irony is obvious enough when we realise that gentleness
seems a luxury out of place on a battlefield. Yet it need

not be for those who are caring for the wounded. Even on the battlefield, the quality of feeling matters because it expresses an attitude towards human beings and an affirmation which become all the more important under such circumstances.

'No man is an island . . .' insists John Donne in one of his Devotions. Although most people agree with this truth, in *The Silver Tassie* O'Casey sharply questions it. Instead, each man can, if he wishes, be his own island. In this way he can realise whatever he can of the life force fundamental to his existence. Unfortunately, this may mean turning the other cheek, accepting injustice, or unfairly enduring pain. But as Act II reveals, when so much happens that lies beyond the control of any individual, it becomes all the more necessary for people to accept the fullest possible responsibility for the condition of their lives. Very few, of course, do; instead most accept helplessness as a reality or even exploit it. For this reason those few who can resist are the more valuable. Yet they can't trumpet their actions; for the others have a right to enjoy their limitations.

Or, to put what I am saying somewhat differently, *The Silver Tassie* makes abundantly clear how little responsibility most people exercise over their own lives, let alone other people's. But precisely because under such circumstances a few people, such as the soldiers in Act II or Harry and his blind comrade Teddy at the end, do act responsibly, these small actions become all the more significant. Yet at the same time those who perform them have to respect others' efforts to derive whatever joy they can from their own lives. For all such efforts, however cunning and cowardly (as in the case of Sylvester and Simon) or sanctimonious (as in the case of Susie), help preserve those admittedly more impressive values of Harry in Act I and of the soldiers in Act II.

The world of the play in Acts III and IV, as Ronald Bryden points out in his review of the 1969 London revival,[36] is so much smaller than that of the preceding two acts. But the result of the difference need not be, as Bryden argues, that the play loses its subject or falls apart. Instead the opposite occurs. Because O'Casey reveres the energy of Harry and the soldiers, he values whatever efforts people make, however limited and mean they may be, to preserve this energy. It would be so much better if the life force, as it expresses itself in those who survive, could be as exciting and as strong as it is in Harry and the soldiers, or that those who survive could have the vitality and joy of Harry and the soldiers, but they don't; and, however much O'Casey regrets this and makes their absence painfully evident in Acts III and IV, he is determined to preserve whatever evidence of these values still remains. If the result is a much smaller affirmation than that of Acts I and II, at least it recognises that human beings can adapt to change and even initiate it, rather than, as they do in the Dublin plays, ignore it or submit to it.

The tone of the play is very bitter, and nothing crystallises this feeling better than a comment O'Casey himself made in the margin of two earlier versions of the play (now in the Berg Collection of the New York Public Library). 'Religion has shown me the hollowness of life; life has shown me the hollowness of religion.'[37] Yet as the play reveals in its very preoccupation with the narrow world of Acts III and IV, O'Casey insists upon plumbing this bitterness to its very depths.

WITHIN THE GATES

In the years following *The Silver Tassie*, O'Casey, as his autobiographical volume *Rose and Crown* reveals, was trying to crystallise his many impressions of England of the Depression years in a play that had many cinematic qualities :

> At this time, he (O'Casey) had become a little interested in the film, and had thought of this play as a film of Hyde Park. He thought the film world was dangerously indifferent to the life of England and her people. He thought of the film as geometrical and emotional, the emotion of the living characters to be shown against their own patterns and the patterns of the park. It was to begin at dawn with the opening of the gates and end at midnight as they closed again to the twelve chimes of Big Ben striking softly in the distance.[38]

Within the Gates expresses this concern and one that is very easy to understand, considering what the Depression years were like in England. Just the barest recital of unemployment statistics—12 per cent in 1929, 27 per cent in 1931,[39]—presents dramatic evidence of how much misery the English middle and lower classes endured. Knowing O'Casey's own experience of poverty and his radical politics, it would be clear why he should concern himself with this misery. However, misery or literally (Latin) *miserere* has a more comprehensive meaning for O'Casey. It embraces a whole complex of attitudes and forces that stifle man's capacity for joy, reverence, and appreciation of sensuous vitality, all of which are much more powerful than they were in *The Silver Tassie*. In fact, these forces are so strong that for O'Casey they could constitute salvation, both in its basic religious sense and in a broader sense to express, as O'Casey often does, the deepest concerns individuals have to make their lives joyous and meaningful. On the other hand, everything that threatens these forces or represents salvation in a narrow conventional establishment manner O'Casey considers a form of misery. And these forces, too, seem stronger and more pervasive than in *The Silver Tassie*.

Consequently, the play in both a strict religious sense and in a much broader context dramatises the need for salvation and the terrible threats to it in the England of the 1930's. Or I could say that England of the 1930's is not just economically impoverished but spiritually impoverished, and that the play presents a vision of how pervasive and terrifying such a condition can be. At the same time, it also considers what hope, if any, exists for a change, or at the very least expresses the urgency of such a hope.

Although the film world may have been dangerously indifferent to the life of England, it is clear from the foregoing that O'Casey in *Within the Gates* certainly isn't. Of all of O'Casey's plays, *Within the Gates* may be the most difficult to come to terms with. On the one hand, the play presents many varied, forceful impressions of life; on the other hand some of these impressions seem stilted, diffuse, over theatrical, and even boring. Yet the play sometimes has an intensity, articulateness, and richness of impressions that can make it overpowering.

To dramatise his pervasive conflict between misery and joy, O'Casey sets his play in a large city park, very like London's Hyde Park, and he presents his action in four scenes, each of which represents one of the seasons. The park attracts a great variety of figures representing widely divergent social, economic, and religious views. The figures appear and reappear as though improvising a vaudeville turn or skit to present their views. The central, dominant character is Jannice, a young prostitute who is searching for a meaningful religious ideal. Jannice, like Harry Heegan, suffers as the principal victim of the forces O'Casey is exposing; at the same time she clearly stands out from other characters because of her courage, vitality, and heightened self-consciousness.

The characters who keep appearing and performing, include two old crotchety park attendants who identify themselves with the ruling upper classes by using the pat slogans of popular journalism primarily to conceal their fear of death and vitality; two emaciated evangelists who seem to delight in burdening themselves and others with guilt and fear of damnation; and a group of soap box religious controversialists, identified by the different shaped hats they wear. The men with the hats, who represent such viewpoints as fundamentalism or pseudo-intellectual scepticism, constantly argue about religion or, in fact, any subject. From time to time these three groups of characters turn up and expound the same stock opinions, or express fears that demoralise them, varied only in examples and topics. Admittedly, they can be boring, but they are compulsive and at times absurd (as Ionesco's characters can be).

Yet important as the improvisational episodes are, they don't constitute the central experience of the play. This, instead, expresses itself in morality play-expressionistic terms and primarily involves the heroine Jannice and, secondarily, an Anglican Bishop, one of the figures to whom she turns in her quest. Melodramatic as it may seem, the latter turns out to be her father. As a young divinity student, he had slept with Jannice's mother, and then had Jannice as an infant placed in an orphanage. Common to both the morality play and expressionistic drama is a perceptive central character who reacts on a higher plane of consciousness than the other figures with whom he comes in contact. Through such reactions, this character searches for some spiritual goal to enrich his life and to resolve his inner conflicts. These conflicts in turn are externalised through type characters who embody different aspects of them. More common to expressionism is an increasing disparity between the levels of reaction of the protagonist and the other characters to emphasise a spiritual, at times even mystical, change. More common to the morality play is a series of meetings between the protagonist and symbolic and/or allegorical figures who represent possible goals for his spiritual quest.

Jannice is a sensitive, intelligent, and articulate person with intense, confused, and unsatisfied religious feelings that embody apparently contradictory needs and aspirations. She has deep seated guilt and fear which drive her in despair to seek grace through absolution and self-transcendence. Ostensibly Jannice feels so guilty and fearful because the nuns who raised her in the orphanage in which she was placed by her father (the Bishop) made her feel ashamed of her illegitimate birth. But her feelings seem too consuming and pervasive to come from one source. Like the young girl in Strindberg's *The Ghost Sonata* she may have, without realising it, internalised many of the conflicting disruptive forces in her environment. Or she may represent a complex of ideas of victimisation which O'Casey wants to present rather than some one with a distinct sensibility that embodies these different aspects of victimisation.

On the other hand, Jannice, like so many of O'Casey's heroines, is a person of innate intelligence, sensitivity, and energy, who feels stifled. As an outcast in a privileged society, she has no opportunity for self-fulfilment, and yet values such fulfilment more than others. If anything, she seems to demand it, though the motivation is not clear.

Jannice in her search for an inclusive religious ideal turns to a number of figures who in different ways embody her two opposing needs. There is the Atheist, who as her sometime step-father not only provided her with a home but helped liberate her, at least intellectually, from some of her fear and guilt; a gardener with whom she has been having an affair and whom she believes loves her and shares some of her feelings for beauty; a Salvation Army officer who promises her grace if only she will regard herself as a lowly sinner; the Bishop who embodies the successful worldly religion of the Anglican Church; and a poet (called in the play the Dreamer) who scorns conventional religion and believes that one can find God in nature through sensuous joy and worship of beauty and in the self through love and independence of spirit.

The Atheist, however, is so self-centred that he wants only to propagate his ideas rather than recognise the force of love and compassion. The gardener just wants Jannice as his mistress and at his convenience. The Salvation Army officer so strongly emphasises self-abasement that he violates Jannice's sense of her personal worth and independence. And the Bishop, at least until the very end when Jannice's courage in the face of death transforms him, won't help her because he fears offending his sister and his respectable parishioners for whom Jannice is anathema. Most of the time the Bishop also fears Jannice's independence and dynamic love of beauty because they seem unconventional and irrepressible. Only the Dreamer comes close to providing an inclusive enough religion for Jannice. He loves her for her vitality, beauty, and courage and inspires her to believe in God, nature, and the self. Yet the Dreamer underestimates Jannice's despair and guilt, which in fact her very happiness with him accentuates. As a result, she has to turn again to the Bishop for absolution and reassurance. Only at her death, when the Bishop finally helps her make the sign of the cross, after refusing her pleas several times, does she experience the peace she desperately has sought.

While Jannice stands out as the principal character who undergoes a genuine religious or spiritual crisis, she so affects the Bishop that he begins to doubt his own ideals and actions. To some extent, he feels ashamed of himself for not acknowledging Jannice as his daughter.

Even more important, Jannice's ridicule of his conformity, timidity, and lack of concern for those who
really need his help, however unconventional they may
be, and her courage in facing death convince him that
she is a better Christian than he. At the end all he can
do is pray for God's forgiveness.

By concentrating on Jannice and the Bishop, O'Casey
wants to affirm that Jannice can be a heroic figure as a
potential spiritual inspiration for all who have the
passion, imagination, and courage to be moved. However
the one person (aside in some respects from the Dreamer)
who can be so moved is the Bishop. In contrast to the two
protagonists are all the others in the play whose unchang-
ing and drab lives show how sombrely O'Casey views
England of the 1930's. Such highly contrasting views of
English life could, as I previously suggested, provide the
basis for a most impressive play; yet at the same time the
play produces very mixed reactions. The main reasons
for these mixed reactions have to do with the Dreamer
and Jannice herself. To what extent are they real as
characters or forces (or both) within the framework of
the play?

The difficulty with the Dreamer is that he may represent something more and less than what I have described.
He may represent something more because O'Casey may
have conceived him as representing some ethical absolute.
For him anything short of total Dionysian joy and
unlimited personal freedom without any compromise
with conventional morality seems almost worthless. Such
a character or personification may acquire a negative
validity if the forces he is opposing are powerful or the
need for drastic change so great that anything less than
a fantastic contrast simply won't do. When we see the
weary, stupid park attendants, or see how Jannice's
mother has almost thrown her life away, the Dreamer's
arrogant and intolerant criticism of society seems necessary. Otherwise nothing will make a dent in people's
minds.

But when the Dreamer insists upon making Jannice his protégé, not to mention becoming her lover, he becomes pompous and even sophomoric. For example, at a dramatic moment when the Salvation Army Officer seems to be getting Jannice to renounce her love for the Dreamer, the latter reminds her,

> Jannice, the Dreamer calls you to the deep kiss and clutch of love, to sing our song with the song that is sung by a thousand stars of the evening!

No wonder Jannice's happiness with the Dreamer turns out to be so precarious that she becomes mortally ill and urges the Dreamer to send for the Bishop.

To a certain extent, Jannice herself creates some kind of credibility gap, especially in her appearance in Scene I and early in Scene II. She keeps changing her explanation for her dilemma as though she had forgotten all that previously happened. Perhaps, as I suggested earlier, Jannice doesn't understand herself and keeps having to define herself over and over. Besides her stereotyped role as a prostitute may be meant to provide her with an identity that doesn't quite fit her. Consequently, she keeps expressing herself through this role but yet never knows if it is real.

Such uncertainty could provide for a very interesting character conception, especially if played by a gifted actress, (such as Lillian Gish in the 1935 New York production).[40] Two scenes in particular come to mind at this point: in one Jannice flirts with the Dreamer and the Salvation Army worker; in the other she upbraids the Bishop for being afraid to help her. In the former she shows a rakish wit, in the latter a talent for excoriation. For example, after the Bishop (who is afraid that Jannice will make a scene) threatens to call a policeman, Jannice really turns on him:

> *Young Woman (mockingly)*. Oh, hand me over to a policeman, would you? I see. Easy way of getting

over a difficulty by handing it over to a policeman. (*She stands up.*) Get back, get back, please; gangway, gangway, there—policemen making a gangway for Jesus Christ! (*The Bishop stiffens himself behind his book. With intense scorn and bitterness*) You and your goodness are of no use to God! If Christ came again, He'd have to call, not the sinners, but the righteous to repentance. Go out into the sun, and pick the yellow primroses; Take your elegant and perfumed soul out of the stress, the stain, the horrid cries, the noisy laugh of life; and go out into the sun to pick the yellow primroses! When you go to where your God is throned, tell the gaping saints you never soiled a hand in Jesu's service. Tell them a pretty little lass, well on her way to hell, once tempted you to help her; but you saved yourself by the calm and cunning of a holy mind, an' went out into the sun to pick the yellow primroses, leaving her sin-soddened, in the strain, the stain, the horrid cries, an' the noisy laugh of life. Tell them you were ever calm before the agony in other faces, an' an' the tip of your finger never touched a brow beaded with a bloody sweat!

(*The horrified Bishop suddenly closes his book, and rises from his seat to go away, but the Young Woman with a vigorous push from her hand, sends him sitting down in the seat again.*)

Such a scene is powerful and yet leaves us with a nagging suspicion that Jannice exists less in her own person than as a force which energises others, most of all the Bishop. For this reason, the core experience of the play may really centre more on the Bishop and his dilemma than on Jannice herself. Besides, as a Bishop he exists more within the framework of society than Jannice. For this reason his conflicts are clearer and more consistent than hers and his concern for appearances corresponds more to that of the minor characters. Whatever the reasons, his ordeal is more convincing than Jannice's. Besides, when the melodramatic plot situation with which he has to contend as Jannice's father, is not a direct issue, he arouses some sympathy and reveals some complexity, particularly in Scene I, part of Scene II, and Scene IV.

Scenes I and II skilfully reveal the Bishop as a special member of the religious establishment. He considers himself free from narrow social prejudices because he can chat in a folksy way with common people in the park. Actually, such folksiness represents inverse snobbishness, for the Bishop regards himself and his Church as superior precisely because he can so fraternise. In Scene I the Bishop condescendingly describes the beauties of spring to some of the people in the park by quoting from the Canticles : 'Flowers appear on the earth; the time of singing of birds is come, and the voice of the turtle is heard in the land—God speaking of Spring friends.' Even when the Dreamer reminds him that not God but a poet is speaking of spring and that the Bishop should give due credit to the poet, the Bishop merely answers, 'God is in all, and God is all things, sir.'

In Scene IV, the Bishop shows himself capable of real and anguished self-insight. After Jannice has exposed him as a hypocrite, he tries to break away from the dominance of his sister, a tough-minded, uncompromising woman—and finally does. Even though Jannice twice asks him to bless her and give her absolution, he can't bring himself to do it, much as he might want to. Nevertheless, he does keep trying and, as I have indicated, accepts Jannice's dance just before her death as a religious act. Moreover, he insists that his sister ask for God's mercy not for Jannice but for herself and him.

Besides the interesting characterisation of the Bishop, the park itself enhances the play. Being so open and large, it attracts a great many types of characters whose appearances, casual at they are, help create a vision of life. There are those, such as the nursemaids and their soldier boyfriends who lead superficial, boring lives, the crotchety park attendants who exist on the edge of despair so that a comment by the Dreamer almost destroys them; and frenetic hopeless figures such as Jannice's mother who keeps disrupting others' lives. There is also an amorphous mass simply called the Down and Outs who personify the fear of death and the hopelessness most of the characters don't dare confront in their own lives. No one explains the presence of the Down and Outs or has to. Appearing at strategic moments and, coming in from various positions, they almost engulf the stage.

Yet however different all these minor characters seem to be, actually they unknowingly reinforce each others' views. Sometimes they all turn out to be snobs, or in Scene IV they become a frightened mob ready to turn on even the establishment figures with whom they identify.

But the park does not merely provide an interesting cross section of English life; it also helps O'Casey celebrate basic energies he values. Each of the four scenes, for example, represents one season in nature, and it is clear from the stage directions that each season has a life of its own. Besides, O'Casey uses the park to present interesting visual contrasts, sometimes just by the way characters move in and out.

There is the strong sensuous appeal of music, song, dance, and choral movement, which accentuate the theatricality already evident in *The Silver Tassie*. On a minor scale the opening choral song creates a light-hearted mood to celebrate the beauty and renewal of life in the spring. On a much larger scale is the effort of the Salvation Army officer and his followers to win Jannice to their ranks. By pulling out all the stops as they play and sing 'Ninety and Nine', they make salvation seem like a cheap circus thrill. In reading this scene, we might feel that O'Casey simply can't resist the theatricality even at the expense of dramatic values. But it is also possible that the most appropriate dramatic value is *this* kind of theatricality I have described.

The most exciting sensuous appeal, however, comes from dancing, particularly that of Jannice at climactic moments in Scenes III and IV. When the Bishop refuses her absolution, despite her fervent appeal and his own inner struggle to overcome his timidity, she breaks out into a wild dance which forcefully expresses her pride in her own convictions and her scorn for the Bishop. That she should then die dancing like David before the Lord (II Samuel 6 :14)—granted that this may be somewhat melodramatic—is also fitting, since dancing does express her vitality and sensuous intensity.

To create striking contrasts, different from those of *The Silver Tassie*, O'Casey employs a kind of leitmotif. The four long scenes consist of groups of episodes, which themselves are made up of very short scenes. A particular episode develops a theme through juxtaposing many short scenes to each other, generally in rapid succession. In this manner O'Casey creates considerable variety in nuance as well as cumulative power from the sheer number of details. A good example of this technique occurs early in Scene I when the Bishop, the Dreamer, and many of the minor characters are talking glibly about the virtues of spring. By shifting the scene from one person or small group to another as characters enter and leave the park, O'Casey exposes many foolish attitudes towards the spring. The climax of the scene comes when two shabby evangelists appear with placards reading, 'Is it well with thy soul? It is well with my soul? Their appearance and questions further accentuate the foolish big talk by reminding everyone of his mortality. Yet the evangelists themselves are being ridiculed for their smugness.

The evangelists might be an apt image with which to end. Though just minor figures, they express some of the fears that underlie most of the characters' lives. At the same time, the evangelists are even more cheaply theatrical than the Salvation Army officer. Consequently, as they circulate through the park, they seem almost like a projection of the fears of many of the characters, as well as their superficial efforts to deal with the basic forces of their lives. Moreover, as they dart in and out, the evangelists do move like characters in a film—a reminder that, besides everything else mentioned, the play, as O'Casey suggests in his comments quoted at the beginning, represents an effort to adapt techniques of one medium to another, and to do so interestingly.

PURPLE DUST

Nothing could be more unlike *Within the Gates* than its successor, *Purple Dust*. This is a play which dramatises the mad efforts of two rich, foolish English businessmen to restore an old Irish castle and to live idyllically in the country. Whereas Jannice in her search for a good life has to suffer and overcome serious obstacles, the two Englishmen simply become involved in one grand fiasco after another. Not only do the Irish outwit them but also lure away their Irish mistresses who were themselves taking the English for all they were worth. No wonder O'Casey calls the play 'a wayward comedy.'

Yet, in this play O'Casey continues his attack on conservative English society. The two businessmen are appropriately named Stoke and Poges, after the setting of Gray's 'Elegy'. Like the Bishop and his sister in *Within the Gates,* they believe in the dead past and are trying to resist change. The Englishmen foolishly envision a good life in their restoration of the Tudor castle and its Irish pastoral setting. They believe in fact, that just as they can buy mistresses they can buy culture, taste, and identify with an ancient aristocracy.

In striking contrast, are the two Irishmen who lure away the mistresses. O'Killigan, is an able, energetic architect in charge of restoring the castle; the other, O'Dempsey, is also energetic and genuinely imaginative. O'Killigan fought with the Loyalists in Spain; O'Dempsey comes from a very old family. Together they represent a more authentic tradition than that to which the Englishmen aspire, but they also feel a strong commitment to the present. Like Jannice of *Within the Gates* and Harry Heegan of *The Silver Tassie,* O'Killigan and O'Dempsey appreciate sensual vitality and beauty. However, they associate these more with the rich natural beauty of the countryside and the grandeur of the Irish legendary heroic past which it evokes.

David Krause describes this combination of nature and myth as nature mysticism.[41] That is a living, religious presence which seems an organic part of the countryside, at least for those alive and imaginative enough to respond.

As a sustained contrast in ideals of the good life that might suggest some new ideas of community, *Purple Dust* seems far too oversimplified. How significant can the Irish lovers' victory be when their English opposition is patently third rate? Once O'Killigan and O'Dempsey begin courting the two mistresses, Souhaun and Avril, the outcome is obvious. By this time (Act III) Poges and Stoke are becoming physically worn out, the autumn floods are beginning, the Irishmen are much more eloquent and vigorous, and the girls are just waiting to walk out anyway because they have previously had five hundred pounds settled on them. Besides, they have all but thrown themselves at O'Killigan's feet.

While O'Killigan and O'Dempsey's ideals are certainly more honest and intelligent than those of the Englishmen, they remain vague, and, at least so far as O'Killigan is concerned, at times even inflated. When in Act III O'Killigan becomes floridly romantic in wooing Avril, such behaviour seems greatly exaggerated because Avril would come with him on almost any terms. Besides, O'Killigan sounds like a refugee from a Synge play: 'Come with me, I say,' he urges Avril, 'Come away from where rich ignorance is a blessing; an' foolishness a gift from God! Come to the house on the hill: the door is open, the fire's alight on the hearth, and the table is laid with a clean white cloth.' Even if we grant that the parody may be deliberate, it seems out of place. Since Avril herself affected such speech earlier in the play, we might expect her to spot it here. But, more important, such conscious parody would make a mockery of the

O'Killigan–Avril relationship, and the context of the scene doesn't support such a mockery. No wonder Poges justifiably sneers, 'When the river rises? Come with me and be my love : Come into the garden Maud. Were ever fools so foolish.' Even if Poges and Stoke seem ridiculous for not knowing they are losing their mistresses, at least they can recognise blarney.

Granted that we can only conjecture, yet I would suggest two reasons for the play's thinness of texture at this point. One is that O'Casey seems interested in exploring other ramifications of sensuous vitality than in his previous plays and that the Irish countryside stimulates him because of its rich traditions and nature mysticism. But in the process he seems to be idealising that countryside too readily. The other might be that O'Casey is trying to create more diversified heroic figures who combine elements associated with Harry Heegan, the Dreamer, and tentatively Jim Larkin, but that O'Killigan and O'Dempsey too easily combine the best of all these different images.

Yet if *Purple Dust* seems disappointing as a sustained contrast in ideals of the good life, it succeeds on another level as a celebration of imagination and energy in whatever form they take. Without imagination and energy, any such ideal seems narrow and debilitating; but with these qualities people can also subvert such ideals or preserve those that have become encrusted as the establishment. On this other level the play becomes a battle of wits between the Irish who subvert English ideals of the good life and the English themselves who preserve theirs through their obtuseness and prejudice. In addition, Poges is cunning enough that he can convert utter humiliation into near victory by adroitly shifting ground. Although my interpretation seems to contradict most readings of the play, actually this is not so. I am simply emphasising that much, if not most, of the play's comic energy centres on Poges and Stoke. On the one hand, they are so foolish that there is almost no limit to their ludicrous ideas. Who else but such fools would condescendingly lecture their Irish mistresses about what the Irish are really like?

> *Basil* (enthusiastically). They're dears. All-I've met of them are dears; so quaint—they are sweet. They need control though; they need control.
>
> *Poges.* I agree. All the Irish are the same. Bit backward perhaps, like all primitive peoples, especially now, for they're missing the example and influence of the gentry; but delightful people all the same. They need control, though; oh yes, they need it badly.

Moreover, because the English can be so obtuse, so convinced of their superiority, and so shameless as to deny even the evidence of their senses, they can sustain such attacks and actually launch their own. Like Simon and Sylvester of *The Silver Tassie,* Poges and Stoke can convert apparent weakness into strength, particularly since they will remain successful *English* businessmen, a role they thoroughly enjoy. Therefore for the Irish to bring down Poges and Stoke, the former need to use every weapon available, and they have many!

The most effective ploys of the Irish are sharp, satirical thrusts, sometimes blunt, at other times subtle, that so incite the Englishmen that they make utter fools of themselves. Early in the play Poges admires one of the end walls in the house as a fine example of early Tudor. Highly amused, O'Killigan proceeds to tap the next wall and ironically insists that it is middle Tudor, knowing that Poges will then play the game of one upmanship with him. And this is exactly what Poges does as he raves about the other end wall by distorting history idiotically!

> Late Tudor this one I'm sure. Ah, England had no equal then. Look at the Lionheart, eh? Smashed the Infidel, smashed him out of Jerusalem into the desert

places. What was his name, follower of the Prophet?
You remember, Hegira, the white stone, or was it
a black stone? Oh, what was the bounder's name?

In another instance when Poges mistakenly believes that
O'Dempsey regards him as a trusted confidant, O'Killi-
gan cuttingly remarks, 'He looks upon you and all
Englishmen as a rascal, a thief, and hot-pulsed hypocrite.'
After Poges in his obtuseness insists this is pure ignorance
—'Where would the world be without the English?'—
O'Killigan intensifies his ridicule, 'The giddy globe
would wobble, slow down, stand still, and death would
come quick to us all.' Even at this point Poges only
barely concedes, 'Well, no, not so bad as that you know,
but near it, damned near it.' Through such tactics,
O'Killigan has exposed Poges' Philistine ignorance and
his rampant jingoism—but the task has *not* been easy.

Consequently, although the Irish are vigorous and
imaginative, Poges and Stoke become the primary source
of the humour either in themselves or in reacting to the
Irish. Stoke, as the lesser character, is probably the
simpler to analyse. He has a more clearly established
social position than that of Poges, since he comes from
an old and honourable family and is an Oxford man.
For these reasons Poges finds him useful to bolster his
own prestige. At the same time Poges can also boast of
his own superiority as a self-educated and self-made man.
At Oxford, Stoke apparently studied philosophy and, as
the stage directions tell us, proudly regards himself as a
philosopher. He has the comic gift of irrelevance, exactly
like the men with the hats in *Within the Gates*. He makes
precise epistemological distinctions at the most useless
times.

Stoke is also amusing because he is sensitive and easily
offended, like a child who cries if his feelings are hurt.
When Poges consistently ridicules him, Stoke tearfully
protests that he has read half the philosophers of the
world and deserves to be listened to. He is also in tears

112

when he has made a fiasco of a horseback riding expedition with Avril. Unwilling to listen to O'Killigan's warning that his horse was highly spirited, when the horse hesitated, he used the spur. Not only was Stoke thrown, but he was also personally humiliated because Avril publicly rode off to a rendezvous with O'Killigan. As a result, Stoke wants to be treated like a sick child tenderly carried off to his bed. Yet Stoke seems more defenceless than he is, for he is realistic enough to see when he has made himself the butt, and sensitive enough to feel humiliated. Never again does he go horseback riding.

Poges, however, supplies most of the humour as the central character or driving force of the play. 'Driving force' is an appropriate word, to use, for this self-educated, verbose, insensitive, but successful businessman constantly tries to dominate every situation in which he appears—and he generally succeeds. He has enough physical energy to do so, as well as an absolute conviction that he is an expert at everything and represents a country that comes as close to perfection as is humanly possible. At one point, when Souhaun needles him for trying to 'ride his high horse' in Ireland, he stormily answers :

> 'I'm not trying to ride my high horse here in Clune na Geera! What is said in Clune na Geera is a matter of very little importance indeed. But every right-minded man the world ever knows, or ought to know, that wherever we have gone, progress, civilisation, truth, justice, honour, humanity, righteousness, and peace have followed at our heels. In the Press, in the Parliament, in the pulpit, or on the battlefield, no lie has ever been uttered by us, no false claim made, no right of man infringed, no law of God ignored, no human law, national or international, broken.

O'Casey's real achievement here is to show how absurd but unshakeable Poges' narrow-minded, imperialist ethic can be. Such an ethic, from a radical perspective, can be destructive enough when enunciated lucidly by authentic aristocrats; put in the mouth of a Poges it represents a grotesque example of Gresham's law that bad money drives out good.

Poges is also amusing because of the way he projects his own feelings into every situation and onto every person he encounters. He fervently believes that if he *wills* something, it must be. Since he has talked himself into coming to the country to live an ideal pastoral life, he *will* live such a life or convince himself that he is. When he and Stoke are shivering before a fire in the raw, early morning, Poges assures Stoke that everything will be all right and acts accordingly. 'We'll enjoy it all; we'll feel younger. The air, fresh air, pure air, exhilarating air will be able to get us. . . . Soon we won't know ourselves. We'll eat better, sleep better.'

From all I have been saying, it might be difficult to believe that Poges could function at all in the ordinary world, let alone be successful in business. He has, however, a talent for knowing when he really has his back to the wall and then cleverly extricating himself by brazenly outfacing everyone or simply switching roles. As a member of his class, he has a stock of prejudices on which to draw. At the very end of the play when Poges seems to have lost his mistress, his castle, and his supposed Italian art treasures, he still can envisage himself as the contrite repentant sinner :

My poor little quattrocento, the waters are about to cover thee! My comfort's gone, and my house of pride is straining towards a fall. Would to God I were in England, now that winter's here!

Ludicrous as his position is, he remains undaunted and almost glories in his misery. Moreover, even if we assume the worst—that the waters will engulf him—the truth is there are many more like him, and they are safe in England 'now that winter's here'. Yet are we to assume the worst? In an earlier manuscript version, Poges just climbs into a box and pulls the lid down. In this version he tries to escape.

If most of the humour I have been describing primarily seems verbal, there is also a great deal that is predominantly visual and farcical. This humour is much in evidence in episodes in which Poges and Stoke try vaingloriously to impose their will on physical objects. If the essence of farce, as Eric Bentley observes, is the interplay between fantasy and reality, then such episodes as that in which Poges insists upon pulling a mammoth roller over his lawn represent brilliant examples of this art. Just as a child sees all objects as extensions of himself, Poges insists on believing that this roller *must* be the ideal one to use because he bought it. In addition if he just used the roller confidently and unsuspectingly, the scene would be amusing enough, because of the surprise involved. But Poges just can't resist trying to dominate everyone, as though his power is limitless. The more the workmen who are trying to hold back the roller plead with him not to use it, the angrier he becomes. The result is a wonderful comic tension : no one can possibly be so obtuse, and yet Poges keeps baiting the trap for himself. Consequently, when he does *force* the workmen to let go, he wrecks one wall of the house and almost endangers his life.

Not only does *Purple Dust* show some of the great possibilities of farce, but also, as Poges' last quoted speech and many other examples reveal, those of parody as well. At the same time we can laugh at the English for using parody so brazenly and foolishly, we have to acknowledge what a great defence against reality it can be.

THE STAR TURNS RED

The remaining three plays in this period, *The Star Turns Red, Red Roses for Me,* and *Oak Leaves and Lavender,* resemble each other probably more closely than the other three so far discussed. The crises underlying all of them are more political, economic, and social than in the other three plays. In *Oak Leaves* it is World War II, in *Red Roses* the Dublin Transport Strike (or Lock-out depending on which historian one reads), and in *The Star Turns Red* the Transport Strike, plus other problems brought to the surface by this strike, as well as later historical conditions of the 1930's. In addition, the vision of a good life seems closer to ordinary life than in the other three plays of this period. The good life may represent a projection or expansion of ordinary life, or the two may keep dissolving into each other.

Of the three plays, *Red Roses for Me* is unquestionably the best and should receive the most attention and emphasis. For this reason I would like to discuss this play last, even though this does violate chronology, since *Oak Leaves* represents a transition from the visionary political plays to the latest plays. While I agree that *The Stars Turn Red* and *Oak Leaves* may be inferior plays, I think most of us have apologised too profusely for these plays, or, as in the case of *The Star Turns Red,* merely let some of Red Jim's rhetoric or his politics scare us away.

In *The Star Turns Red,* as Pat Esslinger points out,[42] O'Casey is trying to telescope two historical situations to provide a context for his play. One is the general European political situation in 1940 when the Fascists were threatening to take all of Europe. Though Miss Esslinger does not emphasise it strongly, the Franco victory in Spain also comprised an important element. Within the play, some of the Dublin poor people involved speak about atrocities allegedly commited by the Republicans (whom these characters consider Communists) against Catholics. In addition, there was the growing power of Hitler, and, more to the point, Sir Oswald Mosley's Fascists parading through London streets and General O'Duffy's Blue Shirts in Ireland.

The other is the terrible Dublin Transport Strike of 1913–1914 in which O'Casey was involved and which, as I pointed out in the Introduction, significantly shaped his political, economic, and social ideas for many years to come. Because working conditions in Dublin in 1913 were appalling and wages abominably low, as even employers acknowledged, the union began to become very active under the influence of Jim Larkin. Before coming to Dublin from Belfast, Larkin had formulated principles of a new unionism (known as Larkinism) which was based on militant action in which almost any means justified the end. Since Jim Larkin was a capable, dynamic, and inspirational figure, he became a powerful influence among the workers and for O'Casey himself a great hero. The employers, rather than trying to better conditions, chose to fight Larkin head on. Under the strong leadership of William Martin Murphy, they collectively agreed that only those workers who signed a non-union card would be permitted on the job. (Apparently the immediate issue which determined the employer's timing was a strike of tramway workers. This seems to be the reason for stating, as some historians do, that a strike came first.[43]) The employers did carry out their threat and would not let workers who refused to sign the non-union cards on the job. Because of this lock-out, terrible violence resulted.

As the situation grew worse, the lock-out became a strike—or reverted to one—and after a while few remembered which came first. To protect the union members from the police, Larkin organised a worker or

Citizens Labour Army of 1000 men which antedated the
Red Army by a few years. (A fact which greatly pleased
O'Casey.) For a while this army did strengthen the union
position and helped the strikers gain support and
sympathy even from British labour. As the situation
became more confused, however, a strong nationalist
opposition to Larkin developed within the union. Consequently, Larkin lost his power and the British, rather
than the employers, became the enemy. For O'Casey and
others this whole series of events which, as I pointed out
in the Introduction, helped lead to the Easter 1916
Rising, was a terribly bitter disappointment. Irish labour
had certainly been beaten. But for O'Casey it had been
beaten because it had fought the wrong enemy, the
British, instead of its real one, the capitalist class. Because
of his experience with the strike and Larkin, O'Casey
identified the Russian Red Army with the same pro-
gressive force, Russian Communism, which, as he
envisioned it in the 1930's, represented the workers' main
hope for a better life. Consequently, any force that tried
to destroy Communism was destroying the working class.

From the 1913 situation O'Casey is emphasising two
phases in particular: the opposition of corrupt labour
leaders to Larkin's policies (material O'Casey himself
wrote about in the Transport Workers paper in 1913),
and that moment when, as Pat Esslinger points out,"
Larkin's army became most active and effective.

The play itself takes place in Ireland in a vague
present when we are to assume that conflicts similar to
those of 1913 have grown stronger, since the Church sides
openly with the Fascists (in Larkin's day the Church
showed more sympathy for the workers). On the other
side is Red Jim, obviously modelled on Larkin, the union
army which he controls single-handedly, and a few
followers, who are better-educated workers. Not only do
the Fascists have an army called the saffron shirts, but
also the support of a right wing coalition, the Christian
Front, one of whose leaders is the Purple Priest, an

important member of the clerical heirarchy. The saffron shirts also have the tacit support of many of the workers, because of the influence of such figures as the Purple Priest. On the other hand, some younger members of the Church, represented in the play by a figure called the Brown Priest, openly sympathise with Red Jim's followers.

The outer action involves Jim's efforts to resist his enemies, within and without the union, who are intent on destroying him. The inner action centres on the conflict within a working-class family in which one son (Kian) is a Fascist and the other (Jack) a Communist, with the parents opposed to both but divided in their sympathies. In contrast to other O'Casey plays, however, in *The Star* the inner action leads to the outer. The inciting incident results from the efforts made by the Fascists (who come to the flat) to get Jack to join the saffron shirts. When Julia (Jack's girl and fellow comrade) taunts the Fascists, the Fascist leader angrily orders her to be whipped. When Julia's father (Michael, also a Communist) tries to prevent this, Kian in a fit of rage shoots the latter. From this incident the rest of the main action results. The Fascists hope, by taking over Michael's funeral in a show of strength, to depose Red Jim (at the same time his enemies in the union are working with the Fascists). But both efforts, as well as a third one, to have Jim arrested at Union Headquarters, fail. Instead, on all three occasions Jim and his army become more powerful. Not only do they beat back police but in a street fight smash the saffron shirts. On the other hand, Jack dies in the street fight.

Most analyses of this play generally stress the predominance of expressionistic elements (and it is these O'Casey added in revising the play). These elements exist in the form of choral chants, anonymous type characters with one line speeches describing their injustices, and heightened self-consciousness and a more rhetorical or poetic speech by key characters. But much of the play's

action and characters emphasise the realism and interplay of tragedy and comedy of the Dublin plays. In a
very funny scene (similar to some of the bar room fighting in Act II of *The Plough and the Stars*) one of Red
Jim's men, a wild fellow named Brannigan, storms into a
meeting where Jim's fellow officers are plotting to depose
him. When the officials won't listen to Brannigan's plea,
he whips out his sword and cows them. More reminiscent
of the Dublin plays, however, are Jack and Kian's
parents, whose battles with each other and opposition to
their children's politics remind us of Boyle and Juno. At
one point the Old Man tries to show how he has asserted
his authority while his wife exposes him for his pre-
tentiousness.

Old woman (*snappily*). I thought your mind was
made up?

Old man. I have made up my mind; of course I've
made up my mind; and once, I've made up my
mind, I've made it up, haven't I?

Old woman. The ground trembles when you're
making up your mind. It frightened me at first, till
I remember it was only a man's mind moving.

Just as important as the similarities in character is a
similarity in situation, and that is, to paraphrase Boyle,
'a state o' chassis'—a period of bitterness, confusion, and
distrust associated with civil war. The war in *Juno* of
course was actual, that in *The Star* is fictitious; and perhaps this difference explains why the earlier play encom-
passes much more life. But such an explanation over-
simplifies too much, if only because O'Casey's political
vision and his purpose in *The Star Turns Red* differ
from those in *Juno*. In *The Star* O'Casey is much more
concerned with alerting people to a terrible danger, that
of Fascism, and at the same time inspiring people to
believe in the dynamic, radical visions, which Fascism

threatens. In *Juno,* of course, he feels that both sides are doing damage to the Irish nation.

Not only is there a great deal of humour, but the confrontation scene between the Fascists and Communists at Michael's funeral reveals considerable delicacy and force. According to plan, the Fascists, led by the Purple Priest, march into the room where Jack is conducting funeral services for Michael. Before the Purple Priest takes over, however, he greets everyone in priestly fashion. Seeing Jack and Julia, he hesitates momentarily, but then addresses them.

As the scene develops, it isn't cut and dried either from the Fascist or Communist point of view. When Jack orders some of the Red Guards to drive out the Fascists, the Guards just stand around uneasily. While Jack and the Purple Priest argue, the crowd drones in the background indicating how volatile the whole situation is. Then the Brown Priest, who believes in the Church's liberal social reform doctrines (of Pope Leo X) and who is friendly with Jack tries to intervene but only with extreme care. Not only is he aware of how uncertain the whole situation is, but he has his own conflict between loyalty to his beliefs and to his superior, the Purple Priest. Even Red Jim's dramatic arrival doesn't necessarily resolve the situation, for the Purple Priest by promising the crowd religious favours almost persuades them to abandon Jim to the authorities.

Admittedly, a later confrontation scene when Jim walks into the Lord Mayor's house, where workmen are putting up Christmas decorations while awaiting word of Jim's expected defeat, does seem cut and dried. Upon his arrival Jim spouts such turgid rhetoric that we expect great things :

Red Jim:
   A silken gown's no refuge now, me lady.
   Tell your beads and smite your bosom, woman,
     for your gilded day is dying.

The trumpet of God, unblown in the hand of
a crawler,
Will ring its news out now from the lips of the
young men.
The sound shall shrill in the drowsy ears of the
guildhall diners,
Chattering the teeth of the big-pursed pagans,
Hiding in the shade of a safely measur'd alms;
Given on the handy holy days of the helping
saints,
To any puling pet that will kneel and bless their
bounty.
The thinkers, poets, and brave men say with us :
No more shall the frantic, wakeful mother watch
Her child's new body shrink away from freshness;
First marked by calm canonical hands with the
cross of Christ,
Then blazon'd with the stigma of tuberculosis.
No more shall the big-nam'd beggars crave over
the eager air
A coin or two from a mounting heap, to give
A rotting child a minute's glimpse of the healing
sea :
The flame in the eyes that see will burn
This useless chaff of charity to ashes !

But all he does is to announce his forces' victory and
quietly lament Jack's death. Yet these details mentioned
don't seem obtrusive in the context of the entire play.
Moreover, the anti-climactic ending, particularly if done
with dignity and restraint, might suggest that the victory
is not easy but rather so unlikely that it has to be muted.
In this way O'Casey can, without letting wish fulfilment
take the place of reality, affirm the value of such a
victory and the need to believe in the ideals it embodies.

In *The Star Turns Red* O'Casey dramatises the need
for a workers' army since other labour leaders are so
unreliable, many of the workers themselves unwilling to

be involved, and poverty is a grim reality. He also shows that the Fascists, except in the one scene where Julia is ordered to be whipped, are neither monsters nor sadists, and that they unfortunately command support for good reasons. They have the establishment on their side, and the workers have few allies.

Nevertheless *The Star Turns Red* lacks the breadth, force, and power of a comparable Brecht play such as *St. Joan of the Stockyards*. It is not because O'Casey's vision is optimistic, whereas Brecht's is pessimistic. Rather, O'Casey doesn't make his conflict credible enough. On the one hand, his Fascists seem to be trying too hard to be vicious and authoritarian. Actually, except in the scene in which Julia is whipped, they simply aren't up to it. On the other hand, we might think that Red Jim is too saintly and optimistic to be a successful revolutionary. But I don't think that Jim's gentleness is the real problem. The real problem is that Jim, except in his speech at the funeral where he excoriates establishment Christianity, does not have a forceful and compelling enough vision to make credible O'Casey's basic idea in the play, that Jim's Communism really can synthesise Christ's basic teachings with Marxism. That is, that on Christmas Eve the star of Bethlehem could turn red.

In addition, while the workers' lives are dreary, their suffering scarcely compares to that of the characters in *The Plough and the Stars* or even the Down and Outs in *Within the Gates*. As one of the neighbours describes Michael in his coffin, he seems more interested in his own petty misery. 'Nearly the same as he was when he was alive; nose a little thinner, maybe; no, not really though when you look into it. (*He coughs*). Oh this cough!'

Two humorous incidents in the play, one in which Julia teases the puritanical confraternity zealot, Joybell, whom O'Casey in a stage direction calls a 'Catholic flag-waver', and one in which two workmen make an incredible fiasco in putting up decorations, turn up in a later play, *The Bishop's Bonfire*. In the later play, however, they seem more directly related to the major theme, though in *The Star Turns Red* they seem more amusing. That a revolutionary play can have such episodes in some way gives it a naive force but also limits its real seriousness.

OAK LEAVES AND LAVENDER

Like that of *The Plough and the Stars,* the plot action of *Oak Leaves and Lavender* reveals the impact of war on ordinary, confused people as they are increasingly confronted with suffering and death. Where the earlier play dealt almost equally with several characters in a series of counterpoint situations, *Oak Leaves and Lavender* concentrates on two characters who dominate the action and to whom the others relate themselves. One is Dame Hatherleigh, a middle-aged, somewhat eccentric, English aristocrat who, while her husband is at the front, has turned her ancestral home into local headquarters for all the civilian defence efforts, including the Home Guard, the air raid wardens and the Land Army girls. Despite her eccentricity, which takes the form of believing that Britain was founded by the lost tribes of Israel, Dame Hatherleigh ably and courageously organises these many activities, a task to try anyone's patience. She is aided by the other main characters, her Irish butler, Feelim O'Morrigan. Feelim, who is a shrewd realistic, and humorous person, has come to England because he believed that he would be better off economically. (He is unaware that his predecessor had been killed in an air raid.) Although Feelim spends much of his time taking care of the other characters, he still tries to maintain an ironical, detached stance. But when his son, Drishogue, and Dame Hatherleigh's son, Edgar, die in combat, Feelim actively identifies himself with the war.

The two sons not only dramatise the impact of the war on the two main characters, but in their own persons, as well as their relationship with two of the Land Girls with whom they are involved, express their ideas about the value of the war and the kind of personal happiness or good life possible at such a time. Their deaths and the conversion of the ancestral home into a factory for war production and therefore its virtual destruction as a memorial to the aristocratic past represent the climax of the play.

Judging from this account, *Oak Leaves and Lavender* sounds like a realistic play. Actually, it contains many of the non-realistic elements characteristic of the plays beginning with *Cock-a-Doodle Dandy*. The house itself is haunted by the smell of lavender, associated with legends about imminent death in battle, and ghostly presences in the form of ancestral dancers appear in what David Krause calls a masque-like prologue and epilogue.[45] These dancers represent a ceremonious but empty past whose values of romantic gallantry seem irrelevent in a war for national survival. The dancers also symbolise death, for when they are present they hear the song of a lavender seller who associates lavender with love and death. Other non-realistic elements include lyrical scenes in which, as in preceding plays, characters express their feelings through song, and speeches of impassioned, stylised prose (such as those in which Drishogue defines his ideas about the war). Both the realistic and non-realistic elements express contrasts of feeling and thought at different levels to explore varying relationships involving war, death, and change.

At first glance, the play may seem too 'talky' and disorganised. Much of the first two acts consist of long set speeches, especially by Drishogue, whose views resemble some of those of Red Jim and the Dreamer. So far as England is concerned, he expresses a highly qualified support for the war. Internationally, however, he supports it as a life and death struggle against Fascism. Drishogue also believes in sensuous vitality, though he seems more interested in the aesthetic harmony of nature. While not as dogmatic as the Dreamer in *Within the Gates,* he does mercilessly ridicule an anti-Commun-

ist refugee who comes to rebuke him for his Communist
sympathies. Granted that the refugee (a Mrs. Tutting)
treats Drishogue rudely, she seems too easy a target for
him to bother with. Yet he flays her.

What also contributes to the verbosity is an elegaic
and precieuse quality in many of Drishogue's speeches.
For example, when his fiancee Monica, with whom he
has just spent the night, urges him to agree with her
that death is not the end, he responds in this lovely
peroration :

> Perhaps not; I only know it means the loss of many
> lovely things : the moving patterns of flying birds;
> the stroll through crowded streets, crudely strewn
> about, that the moon regenerates into silvered
> haunts of meditative men; the musical wile of
> waves racing towards us, or slowing bidding us
> farewell; the wild flowers tossing themselves on to
> the field and into the hedgerow; the sober ecstasy,
> or jewelled laugh of children playing; the river's
> rowdy rush or graceful gliding into sea or lake; the
> sun asthride the hills, or rainfall teeming down
> aslant behind them. . . .

But such a peroration seems esoteric for someone
who like Drishogue will at any moment be going off to
war to risk his life. And the risk is real as his death
later in the play attests.

Structurally, the play also seems fragmentary and disjointed. For quite a while nothing will happen, except
for comic business of muddling through the war; and
then all of a sudden townspeople will begin chanting
angry protests about war-time restrictions. Or there will
be a parade scene in which townspeople bid farewell to
the airmen as they go to report for duty; but then, after
this the airmen's deaths are revealed almost casually.
There is, too, a sharp contrast in tone and style between
the epilogue and prologue, which are meant to be
fantasy. Three couples dressed in beautiful, eighteenth

century clothes dance a minuet; as they dance they express their fears about what is happening to the ceremonious past they value, as well as suggesting the haunting presence of death.

However, it is easy to overemphasise the set speeches, or take them out of context where they are meant to be speculation juxtaposed against very different events. More important, the shifts in form and style may represent an effort to embody a different vision of war than that of *The Plough and the Stars* and *The Silver Tassie*. Unlike the other two plays, *Oak Leaves* does not really question the war itself. Admittedly, this may seem to make the whole treatment of war anti-climatic. But precisely because the rightness of the war is not at issue, the experience of the war becomes disquieting. The reason is that since one is less aware of his commitments, he mobilizes fewer defences. Consequently, the casual may turn out to be disturbing and events may suddenly overtake one. In short, *Oak Leaves* may be portraying some of the more incalculable consequences of war.

As a starting point, notice how the humour changes. Act I has a number of farcical episodes in which people just muddle through the war, an obvious possibility for any writer portraying some of the trivial annoyances of war, or simply using some of the native Cornwall characters O'Casey would know at first hand. But the humour begins to have much more edge and suggests some more serious dimensions of the war. In Act III Feelim tries to play his hitherto successful role of mediator to avoid a threatened confrontation between the Land Girls and a conscientious objector (Pobjoy) assigned to do farm work with them. Since the girls, for all of their liberalism on moral issues, are conventional patriots, Pobjoy's pacifist views enrage them. Feelim, thinking he can shame Pobjoy into patriotism, begins to show off his own knowledge of English history. However, the other people standing by (whom we would think might sympathise with Feelim) can't restrain their anti-Irish prejudice. Instead they denounce him for daring to lecture the British about their history.

But much more disquieting is the sheer attrition that the war brings about : Drishogue, Dame Hatherleigh's son, Edgar, and Jennie, a vivacious, sensuous girl who enjoys her life, all die. On the other hand, those who are least involved survive. It is true that we notice them less than in the Dublin plays, just as we feel less strongly the impact of the deaths. For O'Casey is emphasising not so much the loss as the burden that the old have to bear. Three characters, Dame Hatherleigh, Feelim, and Abraham Penryhn, the father of Monica, the fiancee (as it later turns out, the wife) of Drishogue suffer the most.

Penryhn a puritanical old farmer who abuses his daughter is an interesting, forceful character. Like many of O'Casey's best characters, he is wrong headed and virtually helpless because he simply can't control his impulses in a crisis. Indignant when he discovers that Monica has been sleeping with Drishogue, he curses her out, convinced that he must serve as a divine agent of retribution. But when after Drishogue's death he discovers that Monica is pregnant and that his farm equipment has been damaged by fire, he becomes blind drunk, and even that isn't easy. Given his simplistic mind, he can't comprehend that all these crises could be separate.

Feelim is a good natured sentimentalist who thinks of himself as a tough, shrewd realist. During the first half of the play, he seems (as I indicated) to have enough poise and savoir faire to run all the local defense activities. Though he complains, he really enjoys the job because he can bluster and wheedle if necssary and not have to question what he is doing. But, as he sees the toll that the war takes on Dame Hatherleigh, and how the local people begin to vent some of their frustrations on him, he becomes a chauvinistic patriot who makes wild claims for Ireland. When he learns of Drishogue's death, he vows the bloodiest revenge :

Feelim : That was real kind of you, now Monica. Th' old colour. Ay, a brave oul' flag. Is there e'er a war known to man where it wasn't seen? I'd be obliged to any man who'd mention one. (*He pauses.*) Age has twisted a little stiffness into me; but th' oul' eye is still clear, and th' oul' legs are still sturdy. (*To the crowd*) Yous are askin' me silently what'll I do now, an' will I go back to where I come from? (*With a shout*) Give me steel hat, one o' yous! (*Mark hands it to him and he fixes it firmly on his head.*) Let the grey hair be hid behind it, for steel's a sensible embroidery for an ageing head today. (*Savagely*) Th' damned villains, bloodied all over with th' rent-out lives of child an' woman! They owe Feelim O'Morrigun a son; an' be Christ! old as he is, he'll help to make them pay to th' uttermost farthing in th' blood of their youngest an' their best! Let their bombs explode, an' wreck an' tcar, an' tumble everything! It'll take more than they can make an' carry to punch us out of where we stand to fight them! (*He raises his hands in an eloquent gesture*) Hearts of steel, well tempered with hate, is what we are today— hearts of steel! Hearts of oak don't last; so hearts of steel we are!

Even if we are to see Feelim as a committed person toughened by crisis, the savage fury and tin horn patriotism of his speech emphasise the considerable price he has paid.

For Dame Hatherleigh, however, the attrition is greatest. Though her belief that the English were descended from the lost tribes of Israel at first seems amusing, ultimately such a belief represents for her a refuge from the shock of change. Out of a sense of duty, she carries on like the grand lady as she encourages those who are downhearted. But inwardly she is lost because the traditions in which she believes, as symbolised by her house, are dying. Nor has she anything to take their place, not even her outward stoicism. First, she learns that her husband is killed and then her son. Instead of giving in to grief or protesting, she clings to the belief that something must survive, and that is the cycle of nature whose changes affirm the reality of beauty :

Is the crimson cherry brown? The apple-blossom black? The sky for ever gray? No, no ! The cherry is as red as ever; the apple blossom rosy; and the sky is often blue; sweet lavender rears tops of gentle purple; many a sturdy oak shall strut from a dying acorn; and many a maiden's lips still quiver for a kiss.

But, at the same time she expresses this hope, as though it were a vision, she welcomes death as a release.

To speak of change in relation to death emphasises another important theme, perhaps the most important in the play. It is one that O'Casey presents in visual form through the setting itself, the drawing room of Dame Hatherleigh's country home. The prologue takes us back to the drawing room in the eighteenth century, as couples appear and dance a stately minuet. After the prologue, we see the room as it is in the present. Although still beautiful, it is a bit plainer, because of the war. While in Act II the scene is the same the presence of a blackout curtain creates a slightly jarring effect. But the beginning of Act III produces a shattering change, for the whole living room has been converted into a war plant. Nor has it been done by remodelling or simply thrusting machinery in regardless of the aesthetic effect. Instead, O'Casey makes it appear that from the very beginning the room had such a clear, simple functional design that it could easily be converted into a factory. Yet because the change has taken place so readily the impact is all the greater.

In the prologue's minuet, the three beautifully dressed eighteenth century couples represent a ceremonious past which they would like to believe England needs even now. Yet their anxious, pathetic tone belies this :

> *Second Gentleman Dancer.* Look : The buildings topple like the town of Troy. The flames get wider. The enemy is striking home to England's inmost heart.

> *Second Lady Dancer.* Oh, let's go on dancing and never look again.

> *First Gentleman Dancer.* Look ! There, in the midst of the red foliage, the dome of St. Paul's stands out like a black and withering lotus blossom !

Instead, the delicate language, the dance itself, and the smell of the lavender (which later becomes associated with death, as it pervades the house during the play proper) show how change, the past, and death are almost hopelessly intertwined. As a result we become aware both how precarious our inner serenity is and yet how precious it is. Amplifying these impressions are Drishogue's elegaic tone, and poetic perceptions, Dame Hatherleigh's vision and eccentric ideas about Israel, and the characters' odd sensations about death. At the end only death seems to offer any real hope for serenity and joy.

In the epilogue the dancers return, this time, however, with a slower pace. For they know that the past has receded, the present is dissolving, and death seems to be the most enduring reality. Death, it is true, is lovely, but still disquieting, perhaps for that reason all the more so.

The play still remains fragmentary, for even within its own terms too much happens too quickly or seems too sketchy. The potentialities exist for a play that precariously balances lyrical and dramatic reactions to express attrition. But these potentialities are only partially realised. Still, even such partial realisation may suggest that *Oak Leaves and Lavender* deserves more attention than the one production it has received to date.

RED ROSES FOR ME

To come to *Red Roses for Me* after *The Star Turns Red* is an astonishing experience. For, while both plays deal with the milieu of the terrible Dublin Transport Strike of 1913–1914 and the heroic efforts of a young labour leader to fight for his principles, they seem worlds apart. *Red Roses* is probably O'Casey's best work since *The Plough and the Stars*. *The Star Turns Red*, though a considerably better play than is generally claimed, still is by comparison a minor effort. Although many reasons may exist for such a great difference in quality, at least three come to mind as a start.

One is that *Red Roses* has a much less optimistic outcome. Not only do the police quickly disperse the striking workers but in the struggle the hero dies. A second is that the full meaning of what happened does not lie in the strike and the events surrounding it but in the feelings associated with it. The strike, as Harold Clurman points out,[46] merely releases a great many feelings relating to significant experiences of commitment in the life of its hero. The hero, Ayamonn Breydon, is a young, self-educated worker with a vision of a nobler life similar to that of the young O'Casey as described in the Introduction and in Volumes II and III of O'Casey's autobiographies.[47] In fact, many characters and episodes in the play come from these volumes, where, however, they remain separate. To cite just two examples : Mrs. Breydon in her wry humour, Christian stoicism, and appreciation of beauty reminds us of Mrs. O'Casey as she appears in the autobiographies; and Ayamonn's beloved, the beautiful, devout Catholic, Sheila Moorneen, seems to resemble a Catholic school teacher who inspired O'Casey in many ways but was not involved with him in the Transport Strike. By releasing these feelings associated with the strike, O'Casey externalises Ayamonn's vision of a nobler life.

The third, as already suggested by O'Casey's reliance on autobiographical detail, is that *Red Roses* is a very personal play. Not only is Ayamonn similar to the young O'Casey, but in the earliest existing version of the play, the hero's name is the same as that of the young O'Casey, Sean O'Casside. What is more, as I suggested in the Preface, O'Casey's recently discovered early play, *The Harvest Festival,* significantly resembles *Red Roses for Me.* By releasing the feelings associated with the strike in *Red Roses,* O'Casey is not merely externalising Ayamonn's vision but also his own in those formative early years of his life. And it is this personal vision which dominates the play.

Since the vision does dominate, this explains why so many episodes are only partially, or even tangentially, related to the strike. These include Ayamonn's stormy love relationship with Sheila which is largely threatened because she cannot resist her family's criticism of Ayamonn for his Protestantism and inferior social position (although the strike does contribute because Sheila feels that Ayamonn considers his union activities more important than their relationship); his arguments with his mother about his many demanding activities, only one of which involves the strike; and the opposition of two fanatical Orange vestrymen, Dowzard and Foster, to Ayamonn's active role in their church whose minister, Rev. Clinton, he greatly admires. (Since the two vestrymen as railroad foremen are opposed to the strike, their attacks become more vehement.)

Much of the play also concerns itself with Ayamonn's many friendships with people representing widely different ideals. Rev. Clinton is a liberal Anglican with a strong social conscience; Roory O'Balacaun, a fervent Gaelic Leaguer with a chauvinistic love for Ireland; Mullcanny, a religious skeptic who loves to needle the devoutly faithful; Brennan O' the Moor, a quixotic old street musician and slum landlord who likes Ayamonn personally but rejects his religious and economic ideas; and Eeada, Dympna, and Finnoola, three Catholic neighbours who with child-like devotion worship the statue of their patron saint as the one hope for their salvation, yet also join Ayamonn in the strike.

I mention these incidents and characters in some detail because they contribute significantly to the play's meaning. If these incidents and characters meant to corroborate the vision are themselves contradictory and confusing, then what happens to the vision itself? Has it been worth it, since the vision rests upon a firm belief in the great potentialities of a meaningful life for ordinary people.

Like Ruskin, whom he greatly admires, Ayamonn believes that common workmen have strong creative feelings they yearn to express. If given a chance, they could appreciate beauty and sensuous vitality almost as much as Jannice and Harry do, and they could be spirited and independent like O'Killigan. But the poverty, ignorance, and prejudice of slum life here, as in the Dublin plays, make such opportunities virtually impossible without drastic social and economic changes. Like Mary Boyle in *Juno* and the Covey in *The Plough and the Stars,* Ayamonn actively identifies with labour. However, he works much harder than Mary and is much more practical than the Covey. Ayamonn resembles Bessie Burgess in believing in the brotherhood of man as the most significant reality in human life. If Bessie is more passionate and outspoken, Ayamonn is more understanding and persistent. He works hard for his union, and he interests himself in the life of his neighbours by trying to resolve their differences and lessen their misery.

Such a vision obviously is deeply romantic. Not only does it emhpasise the attempt to live by transcendent ideals, but, like that of Yeats, it affirms a belief in the unity and beauty of all phases of life, however contradictory they may be. Nor is this belief in the unity and beauty of all phases of life just an abstraction. It becomes alive through the love of a beautiful woman who in her own person combines many different qualities. For Yeats such a woman was Maud Gonne; for Ayamonn it is Sheila, especially as he envisages her in his favourite song which he wrote, 'Red Roses for Me':

A sober black shawl hides her body entirely,
Touch'd by th' sun and th' salt spray of the sea;
But down in th' darkness a slim hand, so lovely,
Carries a rich bunch of red roses for me.

Her petticoat's simple, her feet are but bare,
An' all that she has is but neat an' scantie;
But stars in the deep of her eyes are exclaiming
I carry a rich bunch of red roses for thee!

The song may also describe Ireland as Ayamonn ideally envisages her in a figure such as Kathleen Ni Houlihan, who in Irish mythology often embodies the contradictory aspects of the Irish character and national life. Such a vision is impressive because it attempts to unify so many different facets of human experience, especially as they are embodied in the everyday life of common people whom Ayamonn knows so well. No wonder he (and by implication O'Casey himself) should ask: has it been worth it? . . .

O'Casey explores the question—has it been worth it— by dramatising the interplay of Ayamonn's vision and the reality of the situation out of which it has grown and which it tries to encompass. The interplay seems obvious and yet turns out to be elusive and ambiguous. On the one hand, Ayamonn openly enunciates his beliefs and tries to justify them in relation to what is happening around him. But what is happening so combines hope-disappointment, success-failure, or contradicts these on one plane and yet corroborates them on another, that it is difficult to assess their meaning and value. Furthermore, there is such a temptation to polarise feelings one way or another because particular incidents or reactions seem to represent an epiphany or the characters involved assume they do. Yet O'Casey to his credit simply won't let us polarise our feelings because to do so violates the nature of the experience he is dramatising.

To mention *epiphany* indicates that the play depends more upon mood and impressions of heightened feeling rather than dramatic episodes. O'Casey simply will *not* let particular episodes, such as the battle with the police and Ayamonn's death, become intensely dramatic. Instead, they remain as stylised tableaux in which the most important thing is the attempt to distil the essence of the experience through contrasting lyrical impressions.

While the play takes place in a recognisable past that seems remote, it also involves the present because O'Casey carefully filters through his imagination these memories on which the play is based. For this reason he no longer has to repress the memories or feel the pressure to resolve conflicts immediately. Like Proust, he can create delicate and jewel-like impressions which he then can savour. But the question is whether O'Casey doesn't pay a price since he no longer has to feel the pain and struggle involved? As we consider the play in more detail, we see in each act how beautifully O'Casey reveals the anguish and ambiguity involved in assessing Ayamonn's vision. Yet in the process has O'Casey given up something valuable?

Act I creates a mood of uncertainty that hovers between too easy assurance on Ayamonn's part and half-recognised doubts. He confidently articulates his beliefs and yet finds real opposition and frustration whose strength he may be underestimating. His mother criticises his efforts at creative self-fulfilment because she feels them to be too impractical in the face of more important economic realities. She also criticises the way he idealises Sheila because he ignores the obvious religious and social differences which separate them.

What is more, Sheila herself seems to confirm Mrs. Breydon's apprehensions. She breaks a date with Ayamonn on the one day in the month he is free because her parents insist that she go on a religious retreat. Sheila also feels even more strongly than Mrs. Breydon that Ayamonn's painting, acting, and reading are foolish because they ignore the realities of everyday life. And the truth is much of the time Ayamonn *does* sound like a soft-headed idealist. Notice how cavalierly he dismisses his mother's objection that Sheila would never dare question the Church's authority :

> And who wants to test the Pope's pronouncement? Life and all her vital changes 'll go on testing everything, even to the Pope's pronouncement. D' ye think I've laboured as I have, an' am labourin' now, to furnish myself with some of the greatness of the mighty minds of the past, just to sink down into passive acceptance of the Pope's pronouncement? Let the girl believe what she may, reverence what she can : it's her own use of her own mind. That she is fair to look upon, charming to talk with, and a dear companion, is well and away enough for me, were she even a believer in Mumbo Jumbo, and had a totem pole in her front garden.

Besides being harassed by Sheila and his mother, Ayamonn has to contend with his friends, whose ignorance is appalling. Like Uncle Peter in *The Plough and the Stars,* Roory is militantly provincial. He stubbornly insists that everything must be judged only in relation to Irish nationalism. When Eeada, Dympna, and Finnoola discover that the statue of their patron saint is missing, they act like lost children. Brennan regards Ayamonn and his neighbours as close personal friends whom he likes as fellow Christians; yet he gouges his tenants who live in other slums.

As each of the persons mentioned keeps barging in on Ayamonn, very much like the neighbours in Act I of

The Shadow of a Gunman, Ayamonn's position seems
more tenuous and his protestations of his faith in his
ideals seem too optimistic. Yet one reason Ayamonn
and his mother can argue so candidly is that they *do*
care deeply for one another and their neighbours. While
many of Sheila's actions contradict Ayamonn's idealistic
vision of her, she obviously has beauty, innate good taste,
and deep affection for Ayamonn. And Brennan, despite
all his quirks and contradictions, has a real zest for
living, an appreciation of beauty, and a capacity for
strong personal affection. Ayamonn's position *is* difficult.
Nevertheless, his patience and his hope that he can
reconcile the conflicts or contradictions in his environment are clearly understandable.

Act II more strongly accentuates the success-failure
motif in Ayamonn's many faceted life and more precisely
defines some of the issues. The religious quarrels become
more violent and destructive as Sheila joins in : the arguments between Ayamonn and Sheila grow increasingly
bitter so that reconciliation seems impossible; and the
strike which Ayamonn blithely assumed could not take
place because the employers would be too reasonable and
decent becomes a terrible reality. Yet, on the other hand,
Ayamonn tries harder to stop the religious quarrel, and
he more realistically understands the consequences of his
beliefs. He refuses to compromise with Sheila : if necessary, he can accept the bitter failure of his hopes in her;
and he quietly prepares for the strike. More impressive,
though it seems so trivial, is Sheila's simple assertion of
human kindness at the expense of her deepest self-
interest. Bitterly angry that Ayamonn insists on striking,
Sheila determines to force the Rev. Clinton and, if
necessary, Ayamonn's mother to stop him. Unable to
persuade the minister, Sheila goes looking for Mrs.
Breydon (who is in the next room). A moment later,
however, Sheila returns to say, 'she's stretched out worn
and wan, fast asleep and I hadn't the heart to awaken
her.' This kind of incident, so slight and crazy in its logic

as far as Sheila is concerned, still represents an epiphany which helps vindicate Ayamonn's faith. Yet it is *only* this and no more.

Act III, which occurs at an entrance to a bridge across the River Liffey, reveals both a more limited and yet comprehensive interplay between vision and reality, and it does so in more lyrical terms. It is more limited because it relates more directly to the strike as Ayamonn persuades Eeada, Dympna, Finnoola, and some of their friends, all of whom are dispirited beggars, to join in the strike. The interplay is more comprehensive, however, because it forcefully shows the need for Ayamonn's vision, limited as its impact may be, on the lives of these beggars, and its great superiority to the reactions of others who witness the beggars' misery. The act is more lyrical because it primarily emphasises the characters' emotional reaction to the misery which they witness or experience. Eeada, Dympna, and Finnoola seem almost torpid as they reminisce about their happy girlhoods and complain about their present life in their ugly city. They don't realise that the articulate, poetic way in which they complain reveals that they can still respond to beauty. On the other hand, they don't realise that they indulge in too much self-pity by sentimentalising their girlhoods.

Three visitors who stroll by represent further variations on vision and reality. Police Inspector Finglas (who is accompanied by the Rev. Clinton) has no vision. He merely considers the scene disgusting because all the people, including Ayamonn, are worthless slime. As he talks about the historical significance of the area, he tries to be tolerant but, when someone accidentally spits on him, he loses his temper and violently denounces all the beggars. Roory, who comes by with Ayamonn, has a narrow vision for he objects to a song that Brennan sings simply because it isn't Irish. Nor will he interest himself in the lives of the beggars because they do not embody the beautiful or heroic Irish legendary past personified for him by Kathleen Ni Houlihan. Roory's Irish nationalism represents an angry refusal to face the ugly realities of the present. Not surprisingly, he leaves Ayamonn in disgust. Although Rev. Clinton also leaves, he does so only because the misery and resignation have so shaken him that he dares not think about their meaning.

In obvious contrast to all three, Ayamonn tries to reason with Roory, patiently yet firmly, but without any success. Through a combination of tenderness, exhortation, and good luck (the sun breaks through the clouds and reveals the city's beauty and majesty), he inspires Eeada, Dympna, and Finnoola to join him in dancing and singing praises to their city. For a short time all of the dancers share in a vision of happiness and beauty that enriches their lives and encourages them to join in the strike. But the vision fades when the sun goes behind a cloud. Once again the city seems drab and the dancers' lives still bleak. Yet having glimpsed another life, the dancers quietly reaffirm their support of Ayamonn as he leaves them to prepare for the strike. Their determination has obvious limits, however, for they are still torpid.

Act IV shifts to the grounds outside Rev. Clinton's church and combines lyrical and narrative elements, although more of the latter predominate. Like the end of Act III, Act IV continues to show how the strike merges with the total life of the people as the church becomes the centre of the action. Not only do Mrs. Breydon, Sheila, and even Inspector Finglas try to use the Rev. Clinton's influence to dissuade Ayamonn from participating in the strikers' demonstration, an attempt in which they fail, but the church itself becomes a refuge for the strikers. Ayamonn himself stirs up a religious controversy in the church because he sent a cross of flowers to be used as an Easter altar decoration. To the vestrymen of the church, Dowzard and Foster, who are also white collar opponents of the union (and who are one-sided caricatures), such an action smacks of Catholicism. Unable to control themselves in an orgy of zeal, they destroy the cross. But Rev. Clinton militantly opposes their efforts to keep him from placing the cross on the communion table. Ayamonn's last request that his body be brought to the church and remain there overnight before his burial further emphasises the unity of all aspects of life. Yet it also reveals how success-failure, hope-disappointment are present even at the end. Ayamonn has died, the demonstration has failed, and Dowzard and Foster vehemently object to the presence of Ayamonn's body in the church. The minister, however, again firmly resists Dowzard and Foster's pressure; Sheila testifies finally to the truth of Ayamonn's vision by rejecting Inspector Finglas' wish that she forget Ayamonn; and Brennan, who admittedly disagreed with Ayamonn about the strike and about religion, asks permission to sing Ayamonn's favourite 'Red Roses for Me.' All of these reactions represent a personal tribute to the human kinship and affection that Ayamonn inspired in others.

In the end, the play vindicates Ayamonn's vision and yet shows how far it remains from being realised. The failure of the strike, the terrible fanaticism of the two vestrymen, the narrow nationalism of Roory, the fear of happiness on the part of the Dublin poor, Sheila's religious prejudices and middle-class materialism, and Ayamonn's death itself—all are crippling and self-defeating. But the successes, and, even more so, the nature and circumstances of the failures, create a stronger impression. Because Ayamonn had never doubted what he wanted, had firmly accepted losing Sheila, had reconciled himself to the strike quietly but confidently, and had even arranged to have his last rites be beautiful, he could define the terms on which he accepted suffering and the significance with which he could endow it. And the fact that Ayamonn appears so much less frequently in Acts III and IV makes it possible to concentrate more on the memories of him that the living cherish. Ayamonn has died but what he believes in endures because much of it has been assimilated by those who loved him most—his mother, Sheila, Brennan, and Rev. Clinton.

Since *Red Roses for Me* concerns itself with a poet and his vision, it is not surprising that its language should stand out. To begin with, O'Casey skilfully individualises characters by their speech. The Inspector (at least most of the time) is curt, restrained, and formally ornate, as though he always has to maintain his decorum as the visible embodiment of law and order. Brennan expresses a gaudy bravado, as if he is playing with his feelings or those of people whom he may be teasing. Ayamonn is hortatory, gentle, and self-consciously ornate, deliberately trying to elevate his speech. Some of the time he over-does it to emphasise his gauche confidence, but at others he shows great discrimination.

Yet, different as the characters are, some underlying similarities in their language give the play its particular flavour. By concentrating on a few details and then elaborating them, O'Casey can create a more sustained impression. Consider how Finnoola poignantly recalls some of the legends of her early childhood :

> What would a girl, born in a wild Cork valley, among mountains, brought up to sing the songs of her fathers, what would she choose but the patched coat, shaky shoes, an' white hungry face of th' Irish rebel? But their shabbiness was threaded with th' colours from the garments of Finn Mac Cool of th' golden hair, Goll Mac Morna of the big blows, Caolite of th' flyin' feet, an' Oscar of th' invincible spear.

Her reminscence is clear and sharp in the very way she groups details and in such images as 'shaky shoes' and 'their shabbiness was threaded with the colours . . .' Both show tender restraint (as though she could be moved even more strongly at the sight of the colours) and yet ironical detachment (as if she were also laughing at the shoes which are too big).

In the second place, I would emphasise a rich evoca-

tiveness of feeling. O'Casey achieves much of this richness by subtle, pervasive symbolism. A good example is
that of the rose, which explicitly reveals itself in the
song 'Red Roses'. The rose, however, also means adven-
turousness of spirit, a willingness to be pricked by thorns.
When Sheila comes to pay her last respects to Ayamonn,
she carries roses in her arms. Just as she is tempted to
abandon Ayamonn as a lost cause, she remembers his
remark that red roses were not for her because she wasn't
daring or imaginative enough to accept Ayamonn's
vision. There is also the symbol of a candle. We see it in
evidence in the song that Ayamonn and Roory sing, in
Eeada, Dympna, and Finnoola's praise of Ayamonn and
his mother for the light (kindness) they have brought,
and in Ayamonn's references to his mother as a candle,
a source of inspiration for him.

Still, the most important characteristic is simply a
tenderness that binds people together despite differences.
This reveals itself in the pervasive use of the word *kind,*
particularly at the very end. Just before Mrs. Breydon
gets ready to leave Ayamonn's body in the church and
accept the minister's invitation to spend the night with
him and his wife, she stops for a final look at Ayamonn
and the church yard :

> She's kind (*She pauses to look at the rowan tree*)
> There's the three he (Ayamonn) loved, bare, or
> dhrenched with blossom. Like himself, for fine things
> grew thick in his nature; an' lather came the berries,
> th' red berries, like the blood that flowed today out
> of his white body. (*Suddenly turning to face the
> church*). Is it puttin' out th' lights he is?

The speech itself combines strong, overflowing love, and
yet a more measured appreciation; out of respect for
Ayamonn and consideration for the others, Mrs. Breydon
insists on controlling herself rather than giving way to
grief.

I mention such an example as Mrs. Breydon's speech last because kindness—personal intimacy, consideration for others, and appreciation of their needs and feelings—expresses what is best about the play. It is true that there is a great deal of unkindness in the play : the attack on Mullcanny, the destruction of Ayamonn's cross by the fanatical vestrymen, and, of course, the injuries to the strikers and Ayamonn's death. There is also apparent kindness that masks selfishness : Sheila begs Ayamonn to forget the strike so that he could obtain a good job that would enable them to marry, and the Inspector concerns himself about Sheila's welfare so that she might forget Ayamonn for him. But throughout the play there is genuine kindness, evident at the very end in Brennan's insistence in singing Ayamonn's favourite song 'as a sign of respect an' affection : an' as a finisher-off to a last farewell.' Although the verger (from whom Brennan requests permission) caustically replies, 'An' what d' ye take me for? You an' your song an' your last farewell', Brennan is neither angry nor dismayed, as he answers the verger and gives him a coin. 'For a bare few minutes, an' leave the door open so's the sound'll have a fair chance to go in to him. (*The verger opens the door.*) That's it. You're a kind man, really.' Brennan sings, and the play ends.

The verger's behaviour emphasises some of the bitterness, the failure, and the sorrow basic to the play. On the other hand, Brennan's actions and behaviour represent the affirmation of personal generosity, however quixotic it may be. In doing so, they crystallise the experiences that O'Casey, through Ayamonn, is recalling. They are bitter experiences because they expose stupid, prejudiced, and mean people. But O'Casey insists on giving each of these people (except possibly the Protestant fanatics Dowzard and Foster) his due. Moreover, he recognises how even in failure, death, and misunderstanding, the characters not only are bound together but, without knowing it, incarnate some of Ayamonn's ideals. As the epigraph, which appears in some editions of the play, pointedly reveals : 'You may break, you may shatter the vase if you will, but the scent of the roses will hang on it still.' In the end, O'Casey's forgiveness and the characters' tenderness for each other make Ayamonn's vision endure in some form.

To express some final reservations about *Red Roses for Me,* may be, to paraphrase the play itself, 'unkind.' Nevertheless, for all the play's virtues, something seems to be missing, and that is the depth, complexity, and passion of some of the earlier plays. I don't mean simply that Ayamonn should suffer more or that Sheila should be as impassioned as Nora in *The Plough and the Stars,* for in both cases this would be to betray the characters' nature and distort O'Casey's vision. But Ayamonn could still be true to himself and yet seem more aware of what he has had to endure and overcome to attain his serenity, how precarious that serenity may be because of the quixotic and contradictory natures of his friends and the frustrating Dublin environment, or simply how infuriated or disappointed he might feel from time to time because of living with these friends in such an environment. Or, to state my reservations in different terms, some of the more tragic, contradictory, and theatrical implications of the play's experience seem to be minimised. We can't ask Ayamonn to have the same vision as Harry Heegan and Jannice, but we can regret that his seems more placid. As a result, however impressive the play's treatment of community may be—or precisely *because* it is impressive *in just these limited terms*—it remains a bit remote. We can admire it but we may not be as deeply involved as we may wish. If the treatment of community in *The Plough and the Stars* is narrower, it may be more compelling because it seems closer, in Yeats' words, to the 'fury and mire of human veins'. And if more uneven and diffuse in *Within the Gates,* it may be at times also more compelling.

Admittedly the comparisons with *The Plough and the Stars* and *Within the Gates* work two ways. *Red Roses* is more lyrical, delicate, and impressionistic than the two earlier plays, as though O'Casey seems more detached and serene. But in being more detached and serene, O'Casey may be more removed from some of the greatest sources of vitality in his earlier works. As a result, though Ayamonn's vision may be more comprehensive and harmonious than that of any other heroic O'Casey character, it may also seem more quiescent. Perhaps O'Casey could filter all these early experiences so beautifully because he no longer had to feel so much of his early suffering. Perhaps also he had come to care just a *bit* less for what Ayamonn and by implication his earlier self believed. *Red Roses* commemorates what has passed or is passing; much of the pain is gone and it isn't necessary or even possible to suffer quite so much.

Or it may be that in *Red Roses* O'Casey may still care as much, but he may be acknowledging that the comprehensive vision of a good life underlying the play simply isn't realisable. If this is so, then perhaps it is best to concentrate on what kind of good life is attainable. In turning to contemporary Ireland as he knew it, O'Casey in his last plays may be making a final effort to ascertain just what aspects of the good life are attainable.

IRELAND REVISITED

The biographical details of O'Casey's third period (1948–1964) are even scarcer than those of the second. Because O'Casey seemed to feel a need to use Volume VI of his autobiography to answer critics, much of this volume reads like a polemic and a not too pleasant one. Still we can make a few surmises, especially since we have David Krause's article (already mentioned in the Introduction).

Although O'Casey was always troubled by an eye ailment (as any reader of Volume I *I Knock at the Door* knows so well), he suffered most acutely in his last years. To read, he had to hold a book practically within inches of his eyes. Nevertheless, O'Casey continued to be productive virtually to his death. He also suffered a terrible personal tragedy when his oldest son, Neall, died of leukaemia. Devoted as O'Casey was to his family, it is easy to imagine how terrible this blow must have been. To add to the pain, there was O'Casey's running battle with Irish critics and prelates, which reached its climax in the controversy surrounding *The Drums of Father Ned*. While this battle was not so famous or acrimonious as that over *The Silver Tassie,* it had its own drama.

Along with Samuel Beckett, O'Casey apparently had been asked to submit a play for the 1958 Dublin Tosthal festival. Accordingly, he submitted his latest play, *The Drums of Father Ned*. When O'Casey received his play back, with notation that certain vague changes should be made, he considered the request a subterfuge. Since there were no marks on the manuscript indicating specific changes or questions, O'Casey felt that the Archbishop of Dublin had used his influence to have the play rejected because of some of O'Casey's anti-clerical criticism in his preceding play, *The Bishop's Bonfire*.[48] In support of O'Casey's position, Tim Pat Coogan states that the Tosthal authorities asked, as was customary, that the Archbishop of Dublin initiate the festival with a Mass on its behalf. But the Archbishop Dr. McQuade refused, presumably because of his opposition to the works to be presented.[49] This forced the cancellation of these works. The Tosthal authorities, however, insisted that requests for revision were the issue and represented their specific reaction to serious structural weaknesses in the play. Niall Carroll, drama critic of the *Irish Press* supports this position.[50] But I would also have to add that Carroll's account of the whole episode doesn't exactly encourage us to accept his credibility for he seems cavalier about a lot of issues.

Since the accounts do conflict so much, it is difficult to arrive at the truth. Yet, even if we grant the authorities' case, should they, knowing of O'Casey's reaction to controversies, have acted as they did? After the bitter attacks upon O'Casey in conjunction with the 1955 Dublin production of *The Bishop's Bonfire* (about which I want to comment in discussing the play shortly), Coogan asserts that the Tosthal authorities could have surmised just what would happen. But still they went ahead. All this discussion so far is independent of the merits of *The Drums,* which are not inconsiderable.

That such a controversy should have occurred so many years after *The Silver Tassie* is all the more regrettable since O'Casey to the very end remained deeply interested in Ireland. But his interest reflects strongly conflicting feelings; as John Gassner has said,[51] O'Casey's work dramatises a lover's quarrel with Ireland. No criticism pained him as much as that of the Irish; yet nothing interested him more than life in Ireland. Even in exile, he maintained active contact with Irish political, literary, economic, and social life. As Catherine Rynne points out in an article on O'Casey's letters,[52] he consistently sent many communications to Irish newspapers urging reforms and changes. After all, Ireland still represented the sources of his deepest feelings and the well-spring of his experience.

Nor is O'Casey's choice of subject in these last plays—Irish puritanism, authoritarianism, particularly clerical, excessive concern for middle-class values, all of which suggested to O'Casey some terrible waste of the human spirit—surprising. Not only had he concerned himself with these over the years, but other Irish writers in exile, such as Joyce, had done the same. Besides, the Irish who remain at home also write about these subjects. To take just one example, a play by the young Irish dramatist Thomas Kilroy, *The Death and Resurrection of Mr. Roche:* in this play Kilroy shows how terrible is the emotional and psychic waste in the lives of a number of middle-aged, sexually repressed Dubliners. While other reasons besides religion contribute, it does play an important role.

Yet is it necessary to prove that O'Casey's subjects in these last plays were those that *most* concern the Irish today? To communicate, writers don't choose their subjects on the basis of a Gallup Poll. More important is the depth and range of their explorations. This is particularly true of O'Casey's last plays which project a personal vision of life distilled from his deepest experiences and feelings.

When we turn to the plays themselves, we discover that many characters, situations, feelings, and dramatic techniques persist from the earliest plays. Nor is this surprising since O'Casey throughout his career has shown considerable continuity. Yet, although not readily apparent, a considerable amount has changed.

While some heroic and rebellious characters remain, most of them seem more ordinary and conformist. Or

perhaps I should say that there is less discrepancy between the heroic and ordinary than in the earlier plays.
Formally, although O'Casey continues to emphasise the
non-realistic, he limits himself more to one area, the
fantastic or the supernatural, which pervade both the
setting and the characters' feelings. The fantastic may
embody sensuous impulses within human nature or manifestations of beauty and mystery in nature that suggest a
transcendent, even divine, presence. If accepted, these
fantastic forces may provide the basis for an exciting,
spiritually satisfying life. But there are opposing forces
within the Irish character which we can also call fantastic because they express themselves in people in a grotesque and exaggerated manner. These are prejudice,
ignorance, or what O'Casey calls the 'ferocious chastity' of
the Irish, which those in power encourage because they
fear their own sensuous impulses. Those in power comprise
the clerical hierarchy (though there are individual excep-
tions) and the dominant local businessmen who are also
prominent lay Catholics. Although in the twenty-five
years that had elapsed since O'Casey left Ireland, conditions of life for many people had significantly improved
and industry had developed, nevertheless, as Conor Cruise
O'Brien points out, the middle class and the Church had
come to play an even more active role in most phases of
Irish life.[53]

The emphasis on the varieties of the fantastic prepares
us for a different setting, although one anticipated in
Purple Dust. Instead of the squalid Dublin tenements,
O'Casey (except in two short works, which have an urban
setting) shifts to rural or provincial Ireland. Certainly this
is a convenient setting in which to explore vital energies
in man and in nature. At the same time, provincial Ireland also reveals some of the most conservative tendencies in that middle-class, theocratic Ireland that, as Sean
O'Faolain pointed out, O'Casey envisaged all the way
back in the 1920's. 'Between extremities man runs his
course,' remarks Yeats in one of his poems. And this is

what O'Casey does in his last plays as he both refines and tests his vision of a better life.

In this last phase of his career there are five plays I want to consider. They include three full-length works, *Cock-a-Doodle Dandy* (1949), *The Bishop's Bonfire* (1955) and *The Drums of Father Ned* (1958); and two shorter ones, *Figuro in the Night* and *Behind the Green Curtains.* Of these, I want to concentrate on two : *Cock-a-Doodle Dandy* as his best work and *The Drums of Father Ned* as embodying a final vision which attempts to encompass, if not reconcile, many of the diverse elements in O'Casey's work. For this reason I would again like to invert chronology and speak briefly of the two shorter plays, then proceed to *The Bishop's Bonfire,* and after that to *Cock-a-Doodle Dandy.*

Behind the Green Curtains reveals to what lengths the secular arm of a repressive clerical hierarchy will go in trying to stifle dissent. The play centres on the efforts of a representative of that hierarchy, who remains mysteriously in the background, to try to force a number of intellectuals and artists into following the church's cultural line. When they refuse, the representative's men kidnap a young girl member of the group and tie her to a telephone pole all night. Just this brief description reveals how crude and heavy-handed the play is, as though O'Casey were shooting from the hip

Figuro is another story. It consists of two contrasting scenes. One shows the waste in present day Ireland through the reactions of two old people who feel a mysterious summons or presence guiding them through deserted suburban streets at night. Although they don't arrive at their goal, they still retain their hope. In the brief exchange between the two old people, O'Casey uses fragments and images effectively and just movement itself to create mood and delicately suggest a possible unity in nature.

The second shows a great transformation in which the whole street changes. Kathleen Ni Houlihan attacks a

Civic Guard and he vanishes in smoke; even Catholic
clergy join in singing; and a birdlike figure enters and
leads young people in a dance. In structure and in tone,
Figuro reminds us of a masque or an Elizabethan Entertainment or Progress. First comes a journey and the hints
of some possible transformation, and then in brilliant
contrast, comes the transformation itself which turns out
to be a celebration.

THE BISHOP'S BONFIRE

As the first O'Casey play to receive a Dublin premiere in almost thirty years, thanks to Tyrone Guthrie and Cyril Cusack's 1955 production at the Gaiety Theatre, *The Bishop's Bonfire* created considerable controversy. It is true that there were no riots, unlike the 1926 production of *The Plough and the Stars*. But for weeks before the opening there were acrimonious press comments and rumblings and on the night of the premiere 1200 people stood in line for some 400 unreserved seats. Critical comments by the Irish reviewers were generally unfavourable, even indignantly so. Six years later, however, at the London premiere at the Mermaid Theatre there was less excitement but a more favourable critical response. For many of the Irish critics the play represented an outrageous attack upon the clergy. O'Casey's programme notes for the Mermaid production would seem to confirm this Irish judgment :

But in Ireland [he remarks] we have an almost all-powerful clergy, and the Roman Catholic Bishops are *ipso facto* the Government of the country. The play shows this in the sham of piety and profile, venomous puritanism, and ignorance of all around, laced into timidity against tradition and clerical authority.

For many English critics, however, the play seemed to have a different emphasis. They regarded it more as an affirmation of vitality and joy in which the Irish workmen gloriously subverted the establishment.

We might wonder whether there were really two plays two bonfires—or whether the play presents such violent and lively contradictions as to justify both responses? Or do both responses show more smoke than fire?

The plot action of *The Bishop's Bonfire* is simple and episodic. It concerns itself with the preparations at the home of a prominent layman, Councillor Reiligan, the richest man in the local village, for the visit of the Bishop, an all too ordinary local boy who has made good. Besides the elaborate entertaining, principally at Reiligan's (where the Bishop will stay), there will be civic welcoming ceremonies and a bonfire at which will be burned all dangerous, heretical literature. Although the preparations themselves are essentially minor—decorating Reiligan's house and transporting the Bishop's favorite religious statue from the railway station to Reiligan's—they do involve virtually the entire community and the establishment, and accentuate a basic value conflict that underlies the play.

That basic conflict is between those who believe in the creativity, vitality, and independence of the human spirit and those who don't trust these impulses but believe, instead, that only paternalistic authority, as embodied in the Church and the local community structure, know what is best for men. The former view is embodied by the Codger, a gnarled old foreman or handyman, working for Reiligan, and Father Boheroe, a young assistant to the Monsignor. The Codger is a saltily humorous and independent person, who believes that man doesn't need the Church to satisfy his religious aspirations. Instead, he satisfies them through such sensuous pleasures as appreciation of beauty in nature or in song and dance. Father Boheroe agrees with the Codger that appreciation of beauty in nature can be an act of religious worship. But he believes that the Church can play a vital role provided that it respects the serious element in worship and the variety of ways in which people can discover God.

The more pessimistic viewpoint is embodied in Reiligan and the local parish priest, Canon (later Monsignor)

Burren. Burren, the more astute and powerful of the two, believes that the ordinary Irishman is simply too foolish, dependent, and hedonistic to take care of himself and perform his religious duties properly. By 'religious duties' he means obeying the forms of religion and preserving the community status quo. Reiligan identifies himself with Burren because this sanctions his economic power, extends his social power through lay activities in the Church, and gives him ready-made answers to religious and moral questions.

In between these extremes but roughly identified with them are a number of other positions. All of these together create a considerable spectrum of belief and action—or fear of action. On a comic plane are three credulous and lively workmen who distort the values of Monsignor Burren and/or Father Boheroe. One is a railway porter who is employed to deliver a statue of the Bishop's patron saint, St. Tremolo (a figure with a horn). When the porter stops for a drink and the horn begins blowing, he becomes scared. In his bumbling way the porter really supports Father Boheroe and the Codger in a plea for freedom but is too confused and fearful to acknowledge this. In contrast to the porter is Rankin, a devout and puritanical Catholic. He prides himself on his ferocious denial of bodily desire and regards religion as properly based on fear. He hasn't the vaguest idea how hypocritical he is or how hard he has to struggle to repress his desires. A third character is a Protestant brick-layer called the Prodigal who seems to parody the ideas of both parties. Always vowing to stop drinking because he believes this will make him a better man, the Prodigal looks to religion to control his desires. In this respect his views resemble Monsignor's. On the other hand, like the Codger, he drinks because this makes him happier and livelier. Unlike the Porter and Rankin, he knows he is confused, but he simply can't resolve his conflicts.

On a more serious plane are the positions taken by Reiligan's daughters and the men with whom they are involved. Keelin, the younger, is a lovely, candid, and compassionate girl who strongly identifies with Father Boheroe and the Codger. She would like to marry one of her father's workmen, Daniel Clooncohy, a boastful, good-natured, easy-going young man who believes he can resist his social betters, Reiligan and Burren. With the help of Father Boheroe, Keelin and Daniel do declare their love. But, when Reiligan and Burren expose Daniel as a coward, he leaves Keelin isolated and despairing.

In striking contrast is Foorawn, the older daughter, who strongly identifies with her father and the Monsignor. She believes in repressing her sensual feelings and her love for her father's steward, Maunus Moanroe, and instead devoting herself to a chaste life as a lay nun. However, it is all she can do to repress these feelings because at heart she is a passionate and expressive person. In repressing her feelings, she is literally withering away. Although she half knows this, she dares not change. Maunus seems to stand between Burren and Boheroe, or, more accurately, he seems caught because he rejects both positions. Intelligent and energetic, he had studied for the priesthood, but abandoned this career because of his love for Foorawn. Even though she gives him no encouragement at all, he works for her father in the hope that she will admit her love. Frustrated in this hope, Maunus cynically rejects any principle in which to believe. He is too intelligent and proud to submit to the Monsignor and too disappointed to identify with the Codger or Father Boheroe. In the end, in a wild, implausible scene, he robs Reiligan and kills Foorawn.

From this analysis and other details, there seems to be evidence to support both the English and Irish interpretations. Although Reiligan dismisses the Codger because of the latter's testy reports to Canon Burren, the old man remains happy and outspoken as ever. He has enough money to survive on and he can simply move to another place to live. While the town celebrates the Bishop's arrival, the Codger lies outside the Reiligan's house drinking and singing contentedly. Nor is he alone; the Prodigal, who has tried to repress his desire to enjoy himself by having the Canon put his whiskey in a holy place for safe keeping, admits his folly and steals back the bottle for himself and the Codger.

Admittedly, Rankin remains a puritan, but he is so confused and angry with Reiligan that he has lost much of his zeal. Besides, the workmen have made such a fiasco of the preparations that Reiligan's house looks like a shambles. And can we take the Bishop seriously after we see his statue? As the stage directions tell us : *'The body is barrel-like, the legs are short and fat, the head tiny, and all is dressed in the uniform of a Roman legionary. The one ecclesiastical sign the figure has is his red hair tonsure.'* There is also a hilarious episode in which Reiligan's son, an army officer home on leave, describes his crazy scheme to resist what he considers to be an imminent danger, a Russian invasion of Ireland. By having jeeps and jeep drivers with walky-talkies posted all over Ireland, he is convinced that the Irish can repel the great Russian hordes. By comparison, Reiligan's petty schemes for tidying up his house before the Bishop comes seem trifling.

On the other hand, these seems to be just as much, if not more, evidence to support the view that O'Casey is strongly attacking the Church, religion, and the social conventions of upper-middle class, rural Ireland. Burren and Reiligan quickly scare away Daniel and blight Keelin's hopes for the consummation of her love. Maunus has become so frustrated in his love for Foorawn and so disgusted by the banality and waste involved in the preparation for the Bishop's visit and the meaning that virtually the entire community is assigning to it that he turns his hatred against Foorawn and himself. Perhaps just as damaging is a comic scene in which Foorawn, for a moment forgetting herself, dances with the old Codger, but then quickly becomes serious. Her serious reflections,

however, seem nonsensical because they are so pretentious, and I think, unconsciously parody some of T. S.
Eliot's lines from 'East Coker'![54]

Foorawn (*peevishly*)
. . . We must fall serious, so that every step will
be a new arrival an' a different departure.

Codger
A lot in that, oh, a lot, Miss : here we come, an'
there we go.

Foorawn (*solemnly*)
But listen, Codger : If we want to go from where
we think we are, we must go to where we can't
get; we must set out early before the dew declines,
before the sun rises, before life's fun starts; always
remembering that joy, within the lights or under
the darkness, is joy under the frock of death.

If we go still further, however, I think we will find
something different from either the English or Irish
interpretations advanced. That is, that the affirmations
of the joy of life and the opposition to the apparently
repressive regime are not as strong or as significant as
they seem or could be. The Codger retains his independence, but he is too old to mount much opposition.
Besides, throughout much of the play he seems to be just
as willing as the others to help prepare for the Bishop's
arrival, and he almost wrecks himself carrying a bag of
cement far too heavy for him. As for the Prodigal, he
may be drunk one day, but on the next he will probably
feel all the more the need for Canon Burren's help.
Although the Bishop's statue mocks him, the statue does
scare the old porter and who knows how many others.

But, most important of all, when we look more carefully at the Church as embodied in Burren, is it really so
terrible? Is it Burren who forces Danny to give up
Keelin or is it Danny's abject cowardice the moment he
confronts authority? Granted that Maunus has become

desperate, yet what kept him from leaving? How could he ever have imagined that Foorawn would admit her true feelings and ask for release from her vow? And yet, as Father Boheroe points out, she need not have felt so hopeless. Why couldn't she have understood that people have to help themselves rather than expect divine miracles? In other words, to paraphrase Juno Boyle again, what can God do when confronted with the stupidity of men? Perhaps even Father Boheroe has absolved himself a bit too easily from responsibility for what happened to Keelin. Without much forethought or understanding of Daniel, he urged the two lovers to defy authority in one grand gesture. Wasn't he too hoping for a miracle?

In other words, while Burren and Reiligan play important roles in what happens, they seem less important than the failings or weaknesses of the people themselves in the community. When Burren rebukes Father Boheroe for encouraging Daniel to marry Keelin, he may be harsh, but is he inaccurate?

> Canon (*quietly to Father Boheroe*)
> You're clever, Father—and sincere, I hope—but your cleverness seems only to make people more unhappy than they were. I'm afraid I cannot commend the way you try to lead my poor people towards illusions. Can't you understand that their dim eyes are able only for a little light? Damn, it, man, can't you see Clooncoohy can never be other than he is? You're very popular with our people, but remember that the love they may have for you doesn't come near the fear they have for Reiligan (*he pauses*) or the reverence they must show for their Parish Priest.

We have then, a somewhat different play from that which either the Irish or English reviewers might have us believe. This is a play which affirms the need for responsibility by revealing how the people themselves contribute to their own dilemma. They do so by reinforcing values of the regime itself. For one thing, they perpetuate snobbishness that undermines opposition. Not only does Daniel regard Reiligan as a powerful man but Keelin herself can't easily renounce her position as Reiligan's daughter to which she reverts after her fiasco with Daniel. Reiligan is bumbling and foolish, but does this justify his workmen believing that by spilling cement on his expensive new carpet they are undermining his power? Reiligan not only remains the major employer in the area but the principal landlord and owner of the village store. By exaggerating the impact of their antics, the workmen can continue to deceive themselves about their own abject position. And we might even wonder if Father Boheroe doesn't too easily underestimate the difficulties just because up to a certain point it is easy to disagree with both Burren and Reiligan. The common denominator in all these lives is that the people live by these very appearances or clichés of Irish life which the regime encourages and some of the characters believe they are rejecting. In this regard, I emphasise a tableau scene in the play when just about everyone gathers in Reiligan's house and sings, under Burren's direction, 'When Irish Eyes Are Smiling.' It is true they don't sing 'Mother Macree', but that would, even in this context, be too much!

Given such a society, even opposition might express itself in clichés and it does in the form of melodrama—the romantic variety in the Daniel-Keelin affair and violent in that of Foorawn and Maunus. That O'Casey was using melodrama knowingly is suggested by comments he made (I think in an interview before the London production) praising the work of Dion Boucicault, the nineteenth century Irish-American playwright, who used the form extensively.

Nevertheless, though the play is quite interesting as a revelation of what it is like to live by clichés, or appearances, there still are other things it might have done, other dimensions of its experience which O'Casey might have explored. Edna O'Brien, the Irish novelist, who herself has portrayed with great understanding young girls like Foorawn, and has pointed out that we never see Foorawn at times when she would feel most acutely the burden she bears because of her vow. For Miss O'Brien this burden would be greatest when Foorawn would be alone with her passion. In reviewing the 1961 London production of *The Bishop's Bonfire* for *Encore* magazine, Miss O'Brien remarks :

> My main objection to *The Bishop's Bonfire* is its evasion.
> Ireland is riddled with guilt and failure and a beautiful dream gone wrong. The arrival of a Bishop (or a Jehovah's witness) in any Irish village could produce more than muddle, it could produce heartbreak and violence and hypocrisy and truth . . . O'Casey may not have wanted to do this, he has every right from their barbarous ill-treatment of him to reproduce the Irish as a nation of muddled nincompoops, but Irish and outsiders may ask for something more.[55]

As a writer whose books are banned in Ireland and who has even been searched to see if she was carrying in her possession any of the forbidden books, Miss O'Brien's comments have special relevance. I would agree with her that some of the more tragic dimensions of the experience and even the more richly ironical ones seem missing. They may, as she suggests, be missing because O'Casey did not intend them to be there. He may not have so intended because he had already written a play, *Cock-a-Doodle Dandy,* in which some one's arrival does produce the powerful response Miss O'Brien describes. Perhaps after having written that play, O'Casey did not understandably wish to return. Like Huck Finn he had, as we will see, been there before.

COCK-A-DOODLE DANDY

The basic action of *Cock-a-Doodle Dandy,* involves the efforts of a group of confused, prejudiced, and fearful rural Irish businessmen and clergy to drive out what they regard as evil spirits casting a spell on them. These 'spirits' include an elegant and exuberant rooster who mysteriously appears and seems to play tricks upon them and do damage to holy objects, and a beautiful, sensuous, and vivacious girl, Loraleen, the daughter by a first marriage of one of the town's most successful businessmen and Catholic laymen, Michael Marthraun. Because Marthraun becomes convinced that the rooster and Loraleen (after whose arrival from London all the mysterious events seem to have started) embody supernatural evil, he tries to drive them away. When he is unsuccessful, he turns ultimately to the local priest, Father Domineer, a ferociously ignorant and dogmatic person who tries to kill the cock and has Loraleen tarred and feathered and driven out.

Though Father Domineer apparently succeeds in his efforts, Michael himself only compounds his misery. Because Lorna, his young second wife, becomes disgusted with the irrational, destructive behavior of Marthraun and Father Domineer and his followers, she and her attractive servant girl, Marion, leave him. At the very end, the forces of repression and bigotry control the community more than ever. Nevertheless, the few vital, intelligent, and gay young people have managed to escape. Moreover, the efforts of Father Domineer to effect a miraculous cure of Lorna's crippled younger sister Julia by sending her to Lourdes dismally fail. While the later episode may seem unrelated to the rest of the play, the belief in miracles represents another attempt to deny the existence of natural, physical-bodily forces in human life, a basic theme in the play.

Formally, the play would primarily seem realistic as a battle between two groups of forces for control of a community. But, while some attempts at such realism do exist, the conflict expresses itself primarily in mythic terms. It involves the nature of basic psychic or instinctual energy as a fundamental force in life and the radically different ways it expresses itself in people. It is evident in the cock himself as a source of vitality for all concerned, whether or not they approve of him. But the energy also expresses itself, though in different ways, in the women who yearn to live creatively and exuberantly, and the men who fear to do so. Individuals on each side may then represent different levels or manifestations at which such energy can express itself. To express these differences, O'Casey deftly uses modes of characterisation which range from realism to extreme caricature and delicate stylisation.

Loraleen seems to be a representational character who embodies passionate sexuality so strongly that she dazzles all the men who meet her. At the same time she also has a more independent and original mind than the others, not to mention a sharp wit and a wild, gay spirit. Marion, the servant, is partly a realistic character, as a direct, engaging person, more casual and conventional than Loraleen; yet she is also a pastoral or folk character, modelled on Maid Marion. As such a composite character, she personifies innocent and natural sexuality which an ordinary girl might ideally express in love. Lorna, Marthraun's young wife, is more realistic in conception than Marion. She would like to be gay and free, but, if authority prohibits her, then she begrudgingly restrains herself. The messenger, Robin Adair, obviously reminds us of the folk character of the same name. As a lover, he represents a more stylised grace than does Marion. At the same time, he is a raisonneur who intuitively understands what is happening and comments accordingly. Finally there is the cock himself. Besides being equated with the basic energy of sexuality and sensuality, he seems to represent a more pixieish and amoral gaiety than Loraleen.

The enemies of gaiety are, with one exception, caricatures of various kinds. As such they embody deeply irrational fears, principally of sexuality and sensuality, but also of authority. Although Marthraun acts more realistically after Lorna has left, this is about the only time he does so. Father Domineer embodies a deeply pervasive fear of gaiety and sexuality at a completely unconscious level. This helps account for his fierce hatred, not to mention his ignorance, of all that the cock and Loraleen stand for. Quite similar to him in his consuming fear is One Eyed Larry, a boy who assists in the exorcising of the cock. Larry takes a fierce delight in the whole process; the more violently he can envisage what the cock stands for, the happier he is. More childish and vindictive in his cunning than Father Domineer, he also has a dirtier mind which he freely uses in making accusations. Irrational in a more literal minded and harmless way is Shanaar, a very old religious quack who believes he possesses miraculous powers. Not only is he ignorant, but he seems like a prissy old woman as he supposedly exorcises evil spirits.

While Marthraun seems more aware of his fears than any of the others mentioned so far, he can't do anything about them. Constantly working himself into a frenzy, he seems almost compulsive in his hysterical reactions. One reason for his fears may be confusion about his sexual identity; he doesn't know whether to worry because he is old and feels insecure with his young wife or (what seems to be more likely) to worry because he feels strong sexual guilt which he can neither understand nor confront. By feeling such guilt, moreover, he can rationalise his own selfishness as religious zeal. Since he has given fifty pounds to help Lorna's sister Julia to go to Lourdes, he believes his action will inspire the saints to cure her. It never occurs to him that his gift was good public relations and a sop to his own conscience. Marthraun also has a child-like desire to try as hard as he can to please those in authority. In his mind, the more he indulges his hysterical sexual fears, the better a Catholic he becomes.

Marthraun's good friend, but also business rival, Sailor Mahan, is the one enemy of gaiety who is not a caricature. Sailor Mahan clearly resembles Marthraun in his sexual guilt and fear of authority figures such as Father Domineer. Yet Mahan reacts less hysterically. Having seen more of the world, he knows how repressive his environment is, and besides, he still fancies himself a ladies man. In a crisis, however, Mahan sides with Marthraun because he is afraid of being independent and defying the church. He opposes Father Domineer only superficially to satisfy his vanity; when Father Domineer applies pressure, Mahan quickly backs down.

What structures the play is the momentum a self-fulfilling prophecy can generate when fantasy and fear become so important that they dominate a reality situation.[53] Admittedly, the reality situation referred to is itself a complex combination of forces which are symbolic and mythic. This means that they can't be literally equated with the subjective fears and fantasies which dominate the men. As the prophecy becomes more 'real', sharp differences develop that eventually express themselves in a ritualistic battle of exorcism. Once the hysterical forces become stirred up, in time the mythic forces in nature become more energetic and the battle is joined. The cock mysteriously overturns pictures, destroys sacred objects, and generally harasses Father Domineer and his cohorts. By having the cock respond in this manner, O'Casey may be showing how the law of compensation works; that is, Father Domineer and his forces are trying to repress natural energies. In turn, these energies express themselves more strongly than they normally might.

Father Domineer's group dash madly around, utilise all the resources of exorcism and enlist the aid of the local civic guard, a group of would-be Keystone Cops. Yet in a series of farcical encounters, the numerical superiority of Father Domineer's forces seems to bring them victory. Admittedly, this part of the play isn't wholly satisfactory because O'Casey doesn't show how finally sheer attrition wins out even in a battle of this kind. Or more simply, the symbolic manifestations of Father Domineer's triumph seem more credible than the realistic, despite the overwhelmingly greater numerical superiority of the fools. For some one who respects reality as much as O'Casey generally does this ambiguity is surprising—and disquieting.

O'Casey regarded *Cock-a-Doodle Dandy* as one of his very best plays. While this judgement is open to doubt, it is understandable why for many this is the best of the last plays. In the first place, *Cock-a-Doodle Dandy* has an appealing poetic suggestiveness which derives from many types of stunning visualisation. Look, O'Casey is saying, is all you have to do, provided you are *unafraid. Just look.* Beautiful forms are all around you. As the cock itself gracefully and deftly weaves in and out with its bright plumage, it projects a beautiful, daring, and joyous image. Resourceful lighting also enhances visualisation, particularly when Loraleen appears. In Scene II she suddenly enters just when Michael and Mahan by loud singing try to ignore the spirits they believe are overrunning the house. '*A golden shaft of light streams in from the left of the road*' and follows her as she approaches the men who, in turn, shrink from her. The light makes Loraleen's sensuous loveliness and vitality even more dazzling.

In the second place, there is rich verbal suggestiveness. This results, as in *Red Roses for Me,* from images in stylised speech patterns. When Loraleen warns two young men who are flirting with her that Mahan and Marthraun will make trouble, she verbally demolishes them : 'The two old cronies will tell you a kiss from me must be taken under a canopy of dangerous darkness.' Even Marthraun himself can define his feelings precisely through images. He agrees with Father Domineer that women are a menace : 'An' it's true—they stab a man with a knife wreathed with roses.'

But there is more than flashing lights and bright images. There is, in the third place, fine emotional balance or restraint through which O'Casey does justice to conflicting values in the play. I admit that some of the time almost the exact opposite occurs, particularly in a scene in which Father Domineer becomes so angry with a lorry driver who challenges his authority that he punches the latter so hard he kills him. It is true Father Domineer does great harm and can be vicious. In this scene not only Father Domineer but the play itself seems out of control. There are other scenes too, as suggested, such as the stupidly farcical efforts by which Father Domineer and his cohorts kill the cock and drive Loraleen out. Through portraying these Keystone Cop antics, O'Casey may really be expressing such a strong contempt for these people that he won't let them win as they very well could, namely through their malice and superstition.

At best, however, as the last scene particularly reveals, O'Casey manages to distil just what the different values or forces in the play represent. Though some may feel the tone is harsh, I think at most it is severe and really just.

After Lorna has gone off with Loraleen, Michael sits around glumly, scarcely listening to the good wishes of Shanaar who assures him that now, finally, he will be happy. All that Michael can do, however, is hope desperately Lorna will come back. The messenger, meanwhile, stands by, not chortling as he might but quietly singing a song in praise of beauty to convince Marion to leave with him. As though in a duet, he flirts with her and she encourages him :

> *Marion: (gently removing the hold of his hand on her arm).*
> Your voice is dear to me; your arm around me near seals me to you; an' I'd love to have——
>
> *Messenger: (quickly)* Your lips on mine!
>
> *Marion:* But not here Robin Adair, oh not here; for a whisper of love in this place bites away some of th' soul! . . .

This restraint complements Michael's glumness and also pinpoints the value conflict—the barest expression of love cannot merely harm but destroy. When Lorna's sister Julia returns from Lourdes, her mission a failure, again the value conflict emerges, and again it is balanced. Julia is dejected because of her own misery and the loss of her sister, her main source of comfort. On the other hand, she is brave and compassionate, able to be concerned about Michael's loneliness.

These conflicting feelings blend into a mood of quiet despair, expressed in Julia's request that the messenger bless her. After he tells her 'be brave', she begs him to say more. When he doesn't, she simply orders her father to take her home. Michael, who has been sitting dejected with his head in his hands, can barely ask the messenger whether Lorna will return and whether he should have been less critical of her. But the messenger gives him no consolation; he only prepares to go. In both of these incidents, the characters *could* say more but don't. Then when Michael, now more openly aware of his loneliness, asks the messenger what he should do, the latter quietly says: 'Die. There is little else useful for the likes of you.' After this, he walks away, playing his accordion and singing a joyous love song in praise of Marion. Michael merely sits there, his head buried in his hands.

In his conciseness the messenger may seem, like Father Domineer in his denunciation of Loraleen, cruel. But is he? To let Michael go on deceiving himself would be more cruel. Besides, by being so concise, and singing, as he is leaving, the messenger is also respecting Michael's sorrow. Robin could denounce Michael and stand over him while singing. But he doesn't. Moreover, the messenger is also respecting *his* own and Marion's feelings. By acting as he has, Robin has made a complete break with what Michael represents, so that now he can do justice to his love for Marion. In this ending O'Casey again uses the technique of counterpoint he employs so well throughout his career to emphasise not reconciliation but dissonance. Admittedly it is more muted than in *The Silver Tassie* or *The Plough and the Stars*, and yet in its way as painful.

Finally, I would emphasise the humour. This reveals itself as an unlimited capacity the characters have for irrational but energetic action. By comparison, such action makes children's responses the epitome of sophistication. Although Shanaar, the old quack, appears significantly only in Scene I, he represents one of O'Casey's triumphs. A misguided fool with incredible prejudices and yet an innate shrewdness that keeps him from exposing himself too openly, Shanaar is convinced that only he knows how to confront the mysterious powers of evil. Significantly, the moment he sees Julia returning from Lourdes, he leaves. At this point he won't compete.

Of all the characters in the play Marthraun, however, is the most humourous—and ultimately the most pathetic in his irrationality. Like many of O'Casey's best characters, he is an ignorant, domineering fool who elevates many of his own desires into moral absolutes. Yet he differs from those other fools because he has no idea of his subconscious feelings and how they may affect him. We see this confusion in his humorous account of the mysterious happenings in his house.

Looka, Sailor Mahan, there's always a stern commotion among th' holy objects of th' house, when that one, Loraleen, goes sailin' by; an invisible wind blows the pictures out, an' turns their frenzied faces to the wall; once I seen the Statue of St. Crankarius standin' on his head to circumvent th' lurin' quality of her presence; an' another time, I seen th' image of our own St. Pathrick makin' a skelp at her with his crozier; fallin' flat on his face, stunned, when he missed!

On the one hand, Marthraun projects his subconscious fears on to the religious figures; on the other, he dismisses them.

More ingeniously, Marthraun can almost induce in himself a state of ecstasy. In this way he feels purified and can regard himself as an innocent babe or a person who has seen a divine miracle. A good example occurs in Scene II when Michael flirts with Marion and Mehan with Loraleen. Carried away by his vision of his generosity, Marthraun tells Mahan that he will settle with him on almost any terms because he suddenly realizes how insignificant money is :

> *Michael: (To Marion)*. In our heart of hearts, Maid Marion, we care nothing about th' world of men. Do we now, Sailor Mahan?
>
> *Mahan: (Cautiously—though a reckless gleam is appearing in his eyes too)*.
> We all have to think about th' world o' men at times.
>
> *Michael:* Not with our hearts, Sailor Mahan : oh, not with our hearts. You're thinkin' now of the exthra money you want off me, Sailor Mahan. Take it man, an' welcome! *(Enthusiastically)* An' more! you can have double what you're askin' without a whimper, without a grudge!

Of course he doesn't mean this at all; it is just a momentary impulse.

Through Marthraun's vivid use of his subconscious fantasies, O'Casey cleverly portrays his confused feelings about sensuous pleasure and sensuality and pointedly exposes his selfishness. Marthraun has such fears about his sexual identity that he is apprehensive whenever the slightest threat presents itself. However, by projecting his fears as shown he relieves himself from having to confront them directly. At the same time he can also justify feeling guilty and strengthen his identification with Father Domineer. Moreover, the guiltier he can feel, the more readily he can convince himself of his own worth. Ironically, he overindulges himself in his overreactions and in this way alienates his wife Lorna. Since he has experienced so much fear and guilt, he feels clearly he should have been rewarded as a good boy. Instead, he finds himself abandoned without in the least understanding how it all happened.

THE DRUMS OF FATHER NED

At first glance *The Drums of Father Ned* (subtitled *A Microcosm of Ireland*) merely seems like a rerun of *The Bishop's Bonfire*. Again a civic occasion, this time the preparations for a cultural festival, provides the plot framework within which we see in microcosm the life of the community. A priestly figure whom we never see nevertheless exercises considerable influence; and again the young generation opposes the older theocratic establishment which has been running the town. When we look more closely, however, we see that this time 'all is changed, changed utterly . . .' By the end of the play the older generation is so stunned by the energy, boldness, and astuteness of the young people that they give in. Equally important, what the young people stand for and what, paradoxically the old do so as well, even without knowing it, represents an ideal of community that significantly modifies many of the conflicts that pervade *Cock-a-Doodle Dandy* and *The Bishop's Bonfire*, and even *Oak Leaves and Lavender*. If *The Bishop's Bonfire*, as O'Casey himself describes it, is 'a sad play within the tune of a polka', then *The Drums* is more of a romp. Or, to use different musical terms, one play emphasises dissonance, the other harmony.

In emphasising harmony, we might feel that O'Casey in *The Drums,* like Shakespeare in *The Tempest,* embodies a final, serene vision. To suggest this, though, is to make greatly exaggerated claims for *The Drums of Father Ned* because it has a much smaller scope than *The Tempest* and some real limitations. Nevertheless, the comparison has some validity because O'Casey, like Shakespeare, is trying to project some of the ways in life and yet joyously accept the stubborn realities of the ordinary world. In both plays there is a metaphysical vision, although much more comprehensive in Shakespeare, and in both a celebration, to use Wallace Stevens' phrase, of 'things as they are'.

Because of the play's intent and the fact that *The Drums* is O'Casey's last full-length work, there is a great temptation either to overestimate O'Casey's achievement or to underestimate the play because most of the time it does not seem to embody such great aspirations. Yet because O'Casey does not consistently reach for the stars but stays closer to earth, he does within limits create an engaging work.

How does O'Casey significantly modify the conflicts pervading *Cock-a-Doodle Dandy* and *The Bishop's Bonfire*, and to a lesser extent, *Oak Leaves and Lavender*?

First and foremost, he does so through the very character of Father Ned. Though Father Ned does not appear, there is no question that he exists because almost all of the characters of the play feel his impact. He may bedevil, bewilder, or inspire them, but, unquestionably, he makes his presence keenly felt. To mention bewilderment and bedevilment suggests the cock in *Cock-a-Doodle Dandy*. And, in fact, we can best understand Father Ned when we realise that he possesses many of the same energies and values as the cock, but translates them into religious terms. Like the cock, he is gay, energetic, and sensuous, and as such embodies psychic energies or impulses common to all people. Unfortunately, many people don't appreciate or understand such energies, or, what is worse, fear them. In *Cock-a-Doodle Dandy*, Marthraun and Father Domineer have an almost pathological fear of such energies and impulses. In *The Drums*, while the businessmen, Binnington and McGilligan, and the parish priest, Father Fillifogue, don't understand these energies or impulses, they half accept and enjoy them. Even in their worst moment when the two businessmen prefer having the British Black and Tans shoot at them rather than give up their absurd feud of many years standing, they half enjoy thwarting the British and indulging their own prejudices.

Father Ned, nevertheless, differs from the cock because he embodies contradictions—or, rather, more contradictions. He opposes much of orthodox religion, yet he is a priest and enjoys prayer and religious ritual. He is an idealist who talks grandiously about love and beauty; yet he is a strange, shrewd, fierce looking man. Instead of being horrified when he discovers that Binnington and McGilligan, together with Skerighan, an Ulster businessman, plan to make a killing by bringing in lumber, which they have purchased cheaply from a Communist country, and unloading it secretly while everyone is engrossed in the Tosthal, he simply urges that the lumber be used in local housing projects. Significantly, the most sustained and vivid description of him comes from the Protestant Skerighan who obviously can't forget Father Ned :

> Not thot way, mon, for there wasna claithin' on a body that wasna there, but fierce green eyes shinin' lak umeralds on fire in a white face thot was careerin' aboot through stayin' stull as an evenin' star, starin' up tae me frum doon in th' valley below . . .

> Aw'y, on' a wild flop of ruddy hair, flamin' lak a burnin' bush; one long white hond pointin' up, th' ither one pointin' doon, forbye th' sound of a clear voice sayin' naethin' on' meanin' all, all surrounded by a michty clerical collar round a neck I couldna see; all th' time, th' green eyes starin' doon at me fraw th' top o' th' hill, on' up at me frae th' valley below that werena there.

This long description effectively reveals the powerful impact Father Ned can make and how his very appearance emphasises contradictions. While both Skerighan and Father Fillifogue, who confirms what the former has seen, are startled by these contradictions, they still accept them.

In presenting Father Ned as such a striking and yet inscrutable figure, O'Casey is trying to synthesise many of the different attitudes and values he has admired over the years but which often conflicted with one another. These include the heroic and anti-heroic, the visionary and the realist, the dedicated reformer and the easy-going hedonist. At the very least, he makes us sharply aware of the value of such a synthesis and begins to suggest it as a possibility.

Second, there is another figure whom we never see but who means a great deal to some of the characters, especially the young lovers. This figure is Angus, the Celtic god of love and beauty. He is not real in the same sense as Father Ned; as representing many of the contradictions of the human condition that religion tries to encompass. Angus is real, however, as a work of art or an emblem may be; as a distillation of beautiful sense impressions that are concrete and yet may stand for—or point to—some higher reality. Angus is portrayed in brilliant colours to suggest sensuous beauty, with birds on his shoulders to suggest high aspiration, and with a harp to symbolise music. As G. Wilson Knight remarks :

> What the emblem asserts is what O'Casey has always been meaning : that is, that within the *essence* of youth-beauty there is a pointer of appalling importance. It is the inward and universal essence that is being honoured, independent of particular forms; and since it has this especial independence, this essence must be posited as an external myth-person, in his own right.[56]

Angus exists not only to emphasise the many facets of sensuous beauty, but also to effect a reconciliation between the transient and the permanent in human relations and in man's response to nature. Significantly, the young lovers, Nora and Michael, the children of the two businessmen, Binnington and McGilligan, most appreciate Angus for what he represents. They become aware of the god's existence as part of nature and their feelings for one another :

> *Michael:* My god, an' we're tangled, too, in life's great glittering braid! To know the stars only through the song of a poet; then to forget the poet and the song he sang! *(He suddenly clasps Nora in his arms.)* All the stars of heaven are close to me when you are near. Angus the Young is by our side; we hear his harp-music, and his brilliant birds are perching on our shoulders.

> *Nora:* For a brief while, my Michael. The purple tint of love must fade, and its passion becomes a whisper from a night that's gone. May our love pass quietly into companionship, for that is the one consummation of united life.

> *Michael:* Yes, the Bard and his harp, with his birds, must go one day, leaving us to live in our own light, and make our own music. So we shall; then take a kiss for what it's worth, and let the dream go by.

Although we know the god Angus only transiently, we also know him (as Knight observes)[57] in a moment of vision. Consequently, such knowledge makes meaningful and enduring our experiences of love, beauty, and companionship. 'Though we cannot', to quote Knight, 'always be on the level where the splendour exists, it is enough to have known that there is such a level and such a splendour.' The rest of the time, we have to live more casually. But we need not regret this. Knowing that these large forces symbolised by Angus and Father Ned underlie our ordinary living experiences, we are free to enjoy the latter all the more. In fact, even if we just vaguely sense that these forces exist, we can still enrich our ordinary living.

In dramatising such a vision of harmony, O'Casey's problem is to find a proper balance in dramatic terms between the large symbolic forces and the ordinary experiences to which they give meaning. If O'Casey concentrates too much on the symbolic, the everyday experience would by comparison become too trivial. If he concentrates too much on the everyday, the symbolic figures would seem exaggerated and out of place or merely superimposed. O'Casey by no means solves this problem, but he does achieve a considerable degree of success. He does so mainly through the antics of some of his older characters who are, as I suggested, closer in spirit to the young than anyone would dare recognise. Or perhaps I should say that the young people may understand more, but the older people respond more spontaneously and interestingly.

One limitation is that the young characters, particularly Nora and Michael, are not particularly lively or interesting. They are too self-confident and self-reliant, too 'cool.' Since their parents certainly don't represent strong opposition, the young people may to some extent feel justified in being so sure of themselves. But, on the other hand, since they *are* their parents' children, they might show some of their parents' reactions or at least oppose these reactions more vehemently than they do. When Nora explains why she and Michael have decided to be candidates opposing their parents in the next civic election, she too easily dismisses all opposition :

You see, Father, we're fed up bein' afraid our shaddas'll tell what we're thinkin'. One fool, or a few, rules th' family life; rules th' school, rules th' dance hall, rules th' library, rules th' ways of a man with a maid, rules th' mode of a girl's dhress, rules th' worker in fields and factory, rules th' choice of our politicians, rules th' very words we try to speak,

> so that everything said cheats th' thruth; an'
> Doonavale has become th' town of th' shut mouth.

She is absolutely right in describing the older generation as fools. In the universe of O'Casey, however, fools
often have a remarkable talent for obfuscation and
opposition.

It is difficult to determine how much the play suffers
because Michael and Nora, unlike Marion, Loraleen,
and the messenger in *Cock-a-Doodle Dandy*, are somewhat one sided. In as much as Nora and Michael
do present important views in the play and their own
credibility as a character affects the significance of these
views. On the other hand, Bernadette, the maid who
works for both the McGilligan's and Binnington's and
expresses some of these ideas, is lively and amusing.

A more significant limitation is that the symbolic value
of the Tosthal seems far to outrun its actual value. In
symbolising the hope for a freer, richer, and more dynamic Irish cultural life, the Tosthal certainly serves a
valuable purpose. As an actuality, though, the Tosthal
is something else. Just as in *The Bishop's Bonfire*, the
preparations are often so minor that they undercut the
larger meaning of the celebration. In addition, some of
the Tosthal events, such as an historical pageant cele-
brating Irish independence, seem boring and pretentious. Admittedly we see the rehearsal for just one incident and the characters' speeches may be historically
accurate. Still, if we are to judge the worth of the festival by the literary quality of the pageant, then, this
speech by one of the Irish patriots in the pageant reveals
we are in for a terrible shock.

> We have stood quiet in our fields, on our hills, in our
> valleys; we have sat quiet in our homes trusting
> the power that held us down would show justice;
> but we have found neither security nor peace in
> submission; so we must strike for the liberty we all
> need, the liberty we must have to live.

This speech shows how poverty stricken are the patriots' imagination and how pretentious are their ideas of the heroes. Yet ironically the speech *is* true.

One the other hand, if the Tosthal itself is disappointing, the desire to be histrionic, to be playful, is strong within the play. It becomes a significant means by which the businessmen and Bernadette reveal how lively, natural, and inventive they are in their own right. Their 'happenings' at least are more interesting than the events of the Tosthal. Although Bernadette sometimes seems no more than a mouthpiece for Father Ned, she can be amusing in her lighter, more histrionic moments. When Skerigan begins making a pass at her, she pretends to be outraged but actually enjoys the whole experience. Bernadette carefully controls the situation so that, although she is sporting with Skerighan, she doesn't embarrass him too much. She adopts a mock heroic tone that puts Skerighan on the defensive but yet enables him to play along with her.

To mention Skerighan, is to emphasise that it is really the businessmen, the fools, who carry the play and affirm the reality of O'Casey's vision of harmony. They have less gall and less grandiose self-delusions. While the businessmen in *The Drums* do accept uncritically the establishment values of conformity and narrow self-interest which O'Casey has been ridiculing in *Cock-a-Doodle Dandy*, they do not fear their own feelings. In addition, because they are not (like Boyle or Poges), outrageously self-centred, they take themselves less seriously. Since they are not as implacable in their opposition to change, their own egos are not as deeply involved. One incident in particular reveals that the businessmen at the height of their folly actually affirm some of the values they are opposing. This incident is the hilarious Prologue or Pre-Rumble as O'Casey calls it.

The time is 1921, just after the completion of an apparently successful raid by the Tans. Exhilarated by their success and wishing to find some outlet for their frustration, the British seize upon the idea of taunting two of their Irish prisoners, Binnington and McGilligan, whose feud is notorious in the community. Even though they have lived on the same street all their lives, attended the same schools, participated in business deals, and are courting sisters, the two men haven't spoken to each other in ten years. As a sardonic joke, the British offer to save the town if the two will speak to one another. But, true to themselves, the two men refuse. Then the British order them to run a gauntlet of rifle fire that forces the two to stick together as though they were partners in a sack race. Even this effort fails dismally because, while the men keep close together, they still crawl with their heads turned away from each other. Even when the Irish patriots finally force the Tans to withdraw, Binnington and McGilligan relish their hatred for one another as much as they do their own safety. O'Casey does satirise the Irish for their prejudice and stubbornness, yet he also reveals that regardless of the circumstances, they are inventive and natural, and that they can still preserve their own lives, and enjoy themselves.

Ultimately, what is most convincing about O'Casey's vision of harmony is not its theoretical and symbolic comprehensiveness. Admittedly, these are important, because they suggest implications in everyday life which we might otherwise ignore. At the same time they permit us to accept such life more easily. Instead, it is the careful limits within which the characters operate that are more important. Granted that the businessmen don't see the folly of their ways and are not converted, the truth is that they don't have to be. Moreover, conditions might be worse if they were because Ireland then would be too solemn.

At its best, *The Drums* doesn't present a final affirmation, just a modest one. While such a modest affirmation doesn't enable O'Casey to end his 'lover's quarrel' with

Ireland, at least it helps diminish its intensity significantly.

Having described *The Drums,* as I have done, it might, as in the case of *Red Roses for Me,* seem unkind to express some reservations about the play. But not to do so would be unfair not only to the play itself but to *The Bishop's Bonfire* and *Cock-a-Doodle Dandy.* The reason is that the very serenity of the play may also suggest just how much O'Casey limits the way he explores his material. It is true that many conflicts exist but, except in one sharp exchange between Skerington and Binnington and McGilligan about religion, they are not bitter or sustained. As Edna O'Brien remarked about *The Bishop's Bonfire,* O'Casey has every right to decide what he wishes to include in his play. But by limiting or muting conflicts, O'Casey loses some of the force and passion that underlie *The Bishop's Bonfire,* which at least some of the times does present such sharp clashes. To return to musical images with which I originally compared *The Drums* and *The Bishop's Bonfire:* if the former play as a romp is more delightful, the contrasts of *The Bishop's Bonfire,* the sad music within the time of a polka, may also in retrospect have their appeal.

CONCLUSION

THE ACHIEVEMENT

Even if we insist upon the harshest judgment of O'Casey's plays, we still have a considerable achievement. Between five and seven of his plays compare favourably with the best or near best in modern drama, and at least half of the rest certainly deserve to survive—and, I think, most likely will. Equally important, all the plays (with the possible exception of *Within the Gates* which has a lot of references that now might seem unfamiliar) still remain theatrically vital and interesting, and could benefit from radically new productions. I include in this list *Oak Leaves and Lavender* and *The Star Turns Red*. Not only did the former play have a brief London run, but the production occurred so soon after the war that details of the war itself may have assumed too great an importance. However, now other motifs in the play might emerge. A revival of *The Star* might emphasise a precarious balance between a hope for some fundamental change and a crazy unpredictable violence, whose potential no one, not even Red Jim himself, can estimate.

Yet *considerable* achievement is not necessarily *major* achievement, for O'Casey during his forty-year career was not a highly productive writer. In this respect, he does not compare to Ibsen, Brecht, and perhaps Shaw, the three I regard as the major modern dramatists because of the excellence of their best works, their extraordinary productivity, and their great influence. (While O'Neill certainly was productive and influential, I would not put him in the same class. I find myself, to paraphrase Eric Bentley, having to try to like O'Neill. As for Chekhov, he remains Chekhov—that is, his four major plays are such rich, complex masterpieces that they give him a stature all his own.) I would put O'Casey in the next group which would include some five to ten modern dramatists just below these first four. Such a list might comprise Strindberg, Pirandello, Synge, O'Neill, Giradoux, Lorca, and Yeats. And if I had to say with which dramatists O'Casey has the greatest affinities, they would be Brecht, Chekhov and Yeats: Brecht for his comprehensive, grimly ironical interplay of the private and public worlds; Chekhov for his delicate evocation of mood and awareness of the complex nature of human frustration and aspiration; and Yeats for his intense, tragi-comic, and poetic realization of sexual and sensual energies. But in comparison to Brecht, O'Casey can be more affirmative, though also more capricious; in comparison to Chekhov, more aware of the irrational and absurd, but less able to present complicated introspective characters; and in comparison to Yeats, O'Casey seems more aware of the consequences of sexual and sensual repression, but much less able to render sexual passion. Beyond this kind of approximate ranking I don't think it necessary or even possible to go.

Clearly then, there are not two O'Caseys—a very great dramatist who wrote about the Irish revolution, and a has-been who wrote about the search for the good life. If we exclude *The Plough and the Stars,* the very best of the later plays still compare favourably with *Juno* and *The Gunman.* I myself regard *The Silver Tassie* as better than either of these two earlier plays. In addition, the continuity between early, middle and late O'Casey is evident because there is a central vision which underlies the plays. At the same time this vision changes : the exploration of a good life in *The Silver Tassie* differs considerably from that in *The Drums of Father Ned.* That there *is* both a central vision and that it does evolve offers further evidence of sustained artistry over a long career, not just a meteoric brilliance lasting for about four years from 1923–1926. I would also mention two other evidences of O'Casey's continuing artistry: the fact that he consistently experimented in various dramatic forms over a period of thirty years, and that his work doesn't reveal a steady decline, with a whole group of bad plays following one after the other.

If there are not two O'Caseys, it is still true that when we consider all the plays beginning with *The Silver Tassie* separately from the earlier Dublin plays, these eleven plays do vary considerably in quality. Only two of them, *The Silver Tassie* and *Red Roses*, can we discuss without making significant reservations of some kind. Consequently, some disappointment concerning O'Casey's development remains as a reality to accept and, if possible, understand. To understand, however, doesn't mean that we must find all-inclusive answers. In fact, to insist upon such will only perpetuate the distortions and half truths that characterise much of the criticism of O'Casey. At most, then, I merely suggest a few possible reasons.

As I pointed out in the Introduction, we can't assert that if *only* O'Casey had not left Ireland and broken with the Abbey, his later plays would have been much better. As Tim Pat Coogan[50] suggests, it is quite possible that the plays would have been worse. Yet to acknowledge such a contingency doesn't preclude the possibility that in some respects the exile and the *Tassie* controversy hurt O'Casey. In this regard I would, again, emphasise his comparative isolation from public life and the theatre while he lived in England. It is true that until his death, O'Casey did maintain an active interest in English and Irish politics, religion, and culture, as his autobiographies, plays, and essays reveal. But apparently for financial reasons, he lived mostly in the country, in contrast to his urban life in Dublin, and, although, as indicated in the Introduction, he still retained an interest in English politics, he was not nearly so active as he had been in Ireland. This isolation, coupled with strong feelings of bitterness also mentioned, shows up clearly in Volumes V and VI of the autobiography.

Besides isolation, O'Casey may also have let his own personal feelings obtrude themselves directly in the plays. From O'Casey's description (in his autobiography) of how he as a youth kept quitting one job after another because he felt that he was being insulted, it is clear how proud and sensitive he was. Given such a basic temperament and the unfavourable circumstances surrounding the exile and *The Tassie* controversy, we understand why characters like the Purple Priest in *The Star Turns Red* or Father Domineer in *Cock-a-Doodle Dandy* are crude and one sided. Besides representing Fascist and puritanical views that O'Casey legitimately disapproved of, they also reminded him of the establishment forces in Irish life most hostile to his own views. In fact, O'Casey remarked to David Krause[59] that he may have let personal considerations affect his treatment of Father Domineer, since while writing *Cock-a-Doodle Dandy,* he was also completing Volume IV of his autobiography which dealt with the exile.

This violent and clumsy distortion of character, together with the equally distorted portrayal of heroic figures like Red Jim in *The Star Turns Red* and the Dreamer in *Within the Gates,* constitute the most obvious defect in the plays. Yet, fortunately, this defect is not too common. What is more common, as I suggested in discussing individual plays, is a thinness of texture or oversimplified treatment of sensuous vitality and its relation to community.

One reason for such thinness and oversimplification may be that O'Casey's vision simply narrows in the plays beginning with *Oak Leaves.* Yet the plays commit themselves to considering a wide range of problems. As Edna O'Brien pointed out in the review of *The Bishop's Bonfire,* what disturbed her was what O'Casey did *not* consider. Obviously, there is no reason that an author *has* to consider many implications of a subject. But all of

O'Casey's plays, with the possible exception of *Purple Dust, do* have a large canvas. Consequently, once O'Casey introduces a character or suggests a problem it is difficult to ignore either. Yet in *The Bishop's Bonfire* and probably in *The Drums of Father Ned* he does seem to ignore some characters and some ramifications of problems.

A second reason may be that the relation between the ideal of a good life and community at times seems ambiguous, even tenuous. Unquestionably, a puritanical authoritarian society, such as that of the theocratic establishment of contemporary Ireland, can threaten an ideal of the good life based on sensuous vitality, and community can become equated with conformity. Unquestionably, too, when the ideal of the good life is as comprehensive as it is in *Red Roses for Me,* it does involve community. For Ayamonn passionately believed that the individual could best express his own creative and humanitarian impulses through involvement in the total life of a dynamic society. There is, though, a legitimate question whether an ideal of a good life based predominantly—or almost exclusively—on sensuous vitality has to involve community. Just by communing with nature, we *can* appreciate sensuous beauty and vitality on our own. Or, even if we grant that the total life of society may affect such an ideal, we can't assert as readily as O'Casey does in *The Bishop's Bonfire* or *Within the Gates,* that sensuous vitality need underlie, or even significantly affect, politics, economics, and religion. In the latter play the unfortunate truth is that, while pretentious religious and metaphysical arguments may be far less exciting than Jannice's dynamic appreciation of sensuous vitality, the former don't preclude the latter. In *The Bishop's Bonfire* we may admire Father Boheroe and the old Codger, but we might question whether their ideal of happiness could suit others so easily.

Or, even if we grant that sensuous vitality can significantly affect politics, religion, and economics, we might feel that the impact would be more complex and difficult than O'Casey often envisages. Conversely, we could also feel that, since politics, economics, and religion can affect sensuous vitality, the quest for such an ideal of the good life may be more difficult and ambiguous than some of O'Casey's heroes, particularly in the last plays beginning with *Cock-a-Doodle Dandy*, recognise. O'Casey reveals great insight in portraying Marthraun's difficulties in confronting his sexual fears; but with the old Codger in *The Bishop's Bonfire* he makes everything so easy that we begin to question what the latter stands for.

A third reason may, as I suggested at the end of my discussion of *Red Roses,* paradoxically result from one of O'Casey's great accomplishments. In not centring the play on the strike itself, O'Casey can distil some of the more lyrical and delicate implications of that experience and of Ayamonn's vision. On the other hand, the actual strike produced far more suffering and bitterness than the play reveals. And such suffering and bitterness are emotions which O'Casey earlier in his career would have emphasised strongly.

In talking to Robert Hogan about his earlier written work, O'Casey made these observations : 'All . . . have gone down into the limbo of forgotten things. But I often wish that they were alive again, for buried in them are a wild joy and a savage bitterness that I shall never know again.'[60] Without trying to question O'Casey's accuracy, I would say that 'wild joy' and 'savage bitterness' are two of the most powerful and profound emotions underlying all of his plays through *The Star Turns Red*. But beginning with *Red Roses for Me,* these two emotions seem less intense and prevasive. Whatever the reasons for this change, and as I suggested in discussing *Red Roses,* they could be both understandable and yet elusive, one result is that some of O'Casey's vital creative energies seem to have diminished—fortunately not greatly, but still noticeably.

Nevertheless, despite these limitations, a very substantial achievement remains, and one that will become more apparent as the later plays become better known in the theatre. It would be salutary to believe that the 1969 London revival of *The Silver Tassie* and the long-awaited (forty-four years) 1972-73 Abbey Production may be a promising sign; but it is still too early to tell. On the other hand, recent events in Ireland, north and south, might help bring about a renewed awareness of O'Casey's timeliness. While as of this writing (summer 1972) the conflict in Northern Ireland hasn't reached the savage intensity of that of 1916-1922 in Southern Ireland, such an escalation remains possible. In that event the vision of the Dublin plays may take on a terrible, new urgency. At the same time in the south, the agitation for sexual and social reform (that the formation of a Women's Liberation Group reveals) may give the latest plays a comparable urgency.

But all such 'iffy' speculation aside, the plays themselves still can compel us, for invariably there are the stark, sudden, and yet delicate contrasts in tone; the blatant juxtaposition of the serious and comic; the loving indulgence and yet rigorous honesty with which O'Casey portrays fools and boasters for whom childhood remains eternal; the passionate and yet tough-minded concern for a better world; the painful awareness of how many wasted lives stand out from the days of the Black and Tan to the present; the consistent sensitivity to language that makes almost all of the plays in some sense poetic; and, especially in the later plays, the bold theatricality, even if sometimes overdone. All of the foregoing embody for me some of the distinctive qualities of O'Casey's achievement.

If I were to try to single out what seems most impressive, it would be his fine sense of proportion. What I mean is O'Casey's talent for boldly exploring a great variety of contrasting elements in human experience without shrinking from their consequences, whatever

H

these may be. For O'Casey sometimes this means accepting impasse and discord as fundamental facts of human experience, with each contrast receiving precise, just attention. Yet it doesn't follow that all have the *same* importance. If this were so, we would have near chaos. Instead, three in particular stand out : the rational versus the irrational; the real versus the romantic and/or idealistic; and the self-seeking versus the compassionate or sacrificial. The rich interplay of these establishes proportion also as the ranking and discrimination of significant opposing forces, not just the random conflict of all.

Yet, if proportion as I have just defined it, means discordia concors, it also means an underlying unity in richly diverse experience. I am referring to O'Casey's deep feeling, intuition, or faith, in community that binds all men together, whether it is a reverence for nature, sheer delight in sensuous vitality, or a feeling of mutual responsibility and brotherhood. At his best O'Casey insists on giving just due to all the forces upon which community can be based. He shows clearly what false or inadequate community, such as selfish need, social status, or simple neighbourhood familiarity may entail. For to deny these is to be unrealistic or foolish. Yet to equate them with true community can be just as dangerous. He also shows that there is an anarchistic self which rejects all responsibility and community and whose strength and persistence we dare not underestimate. At the same time, this very strength and persistence help affirm the reality of community, because to survive under such conditions as the foregoing, is a tribute to the force of community. With great sympathy, O'Casey recognises how chaotic and destructive conditions of life may become and yet how at such times people can act responsibly and compassionately. In so doing, they make Christ's sacrifice a living reality. O'Casey's supreme insight is his recognition that at such moments when men seem most apart they also are most united and that, unfortunately, only at such moments does community fully become a living reality.

APPENDIX

WHO NEEDS REASON:

THE TREATMENT OF THE IRRATIONAL IN THE ONE ACT PLAYS

Although O'Casey's one-act plays span his entire career and significantly resemble his full-length plays in subject matter, structure, and theme, it still seems advisable to consider them separately. While the one acts do concern themselves with commitment and community, they do so more by implication. Consequently, to include them with the full-length plays is to distort them to some extent. To treat the one-act plays with the longer plays would also be to overshadow the former too much, for in their own limited terms the one acts represent a considerable achievement, and one that stands out most clearly when we see them all together. What is more, the very nature of O'Casey's achievement in this short form helps point up some of the strengths and limitations of the full length plays.

The eight extant plays vary greatly in tone and form. They range from allegory or fantasy to naturalism and realism, from farce and burlesque to tragedy or near tragedy. Only two of them, *Kathleen Listens In* (1922) and *Time To Go* (1951), could we really consider bad; while four of the rest, *A Pound on Demand, Bedtime Story, Hall of Healing*, and *The Moon Shines on Kylenamoe* in different ways represent fine achievements. All of the plays—except perhaps for *Kathleen*—show a real sense of control in knowing the limits of a subject, avoid 'gimmicks,' and reveal a considerable range of feeling and ideas, particularly of a humourous nature.

Yet, while the plays differ markedly, they also concern themselves with at least one pervasive theme and that is the role of the irrational. By the 'irrational' I mean the illogical, the absurd, the uncontrollable and/or unconscious in impulse, and their many manifestations and implications in Irish life. Through the treatment of the irrational, we can bring into sharper focus many of the meanings of the plays and appreciate the achievement they reveal.

The two earliest plays, *Kathleen Listens In* and *Nannie's Night Out*,[61] emphasise the more serious, or would be serious, consequences of the irrational. They do so primarily on a communal and national basis as they portray the chaotic period of the Irish Civil War that we find in *Juno and the Paycock*. Of the two, *Nannie's Night Out* is the more serious and more successful play.

Kathleen Listens In is a satiric fantasy revealing the hopeless impasse to which Ireland has come, the 'state o' chassis' to which Boyle keeps referring in *Juno*. One reason is that all of the different elements in Ireland, personified in the play by such representative spokesmen as Labour, Agriculture, Ulster and the Gaelic League, are convinced that only their viewpoint counts. What is worse, they are badly informed. They know only the ragtags and facile slogans associated with their position, and they argue incessantly and fruitlessly with one another for the attention of Miss Kathleen Houlihan. She, in turn, represents Kathleen Ni Houlihan, the Irish legendary heroine who, as suggested earlier, embodies the contradictions and conflicts of the Irish. Kathleen, however, scarcely seems heroic, as she merely 'listens'—that is, idly distracts herself. What is irrational in the play is the outrageous petty factionalism and the ironic disproportion between the legendary Kathleen and actual Kathleen which dramatises the lack of serious commitment and national purpose in Ireland.

The trouble with the play is that, once the characters reveal their particular brand of factionalism, they become boring. They merely repeat themselves and do not interact except to exchange slogans. Kathleen herself, moreover, appears so seldom that the ironical juxtaposition inherent in her character loses most of its force.

At best, the play seems to be a charade in which people are doing entertaining 'bits', rather than sequences of action with sustained character interplay. And, since all the 'bits' seem equally important, the play as a whole lacks proportion and shape. Formally, it is too bad the play doesn't come off, for satirical fantasy is a real possibility in a one act.

Nannie's Night Out dramatises chaos in a much more powerful, somber, and original manner. Written in the realistic-naturalistic manner of the Dublin plays, it portrays for us the grubby, but fascinating world of the Dublin poor. The ostensible subject of Nannie, like that of *The Shadow of a Gunman*, is the contrast between the folly, cowardice, and self-deception of men, and the courage, honesty, and tough common sense of women. In the plot the three suitors of the widow Pender, a shrewd, sardonic grocery store owner, panic when a burglar holds up a store at the very moment they are boasting about their strength and courage. The widow, in contrast, prepares to resist, if possible. She is aided by Nannie, a strong, independent, but crazed and tormented woman who comes on the scene and scares the burglar away. Seen from this perspective, the play is an ironical black comedy in which the widow comes to treasure her independence the hard way. But because Nannie is such a forceful, compelling character in her own right, as well as the fact that a blind ballad singer serves as a bitter choral commentator or raisonneur, the play has a much wider reference.

It shows us the crazy contrasts in life in the Dublin slums, if not in all of Ireland. All three suitors are fearful and self-deceived; but at least two of them seem prosperous, while the third has a sinecure working for the widow. In fact, they flourish because they can't see themselves for what they are or understand the plight of others. Nannie, however, is independent, strong, and brave. Although fatally ill, and at times insane, she so passionately affirms her beliefs that she is willing to die for them. Poverty has made her vulnerable to disease, and society, personified by the police, believes she has to be locked up when she lets herself go. Furthermore, because Nannie is intelligent, she sees clearly how trapped she is. And because she has so much vitality and passion, she has no outlet for her undeniable creative talents. In one ending of the play she dies from a heart attack after the robbery, while in another the police just haul her away to jail for the nth time when she becomes her high-spirited self. From Nannie's perspective, the slum world seems nightmarish with everything distorted and insidiously related. Worst of all, Nannie suffers the most and leads the most hopeless life precisely because she understands so passionately.

Clearly from this perspective, the irrational is more terrifying and pervasive than in *Kathleen*. From the point of view of the widow, however, this is not quite so. In contrast to Nannie who has a sickly son whom she neglects, the widow has her health and her store, not to mention the suitors who constitute a very different kind of threat from all the environmental forces acting on Nannie. Consequently, the widow can reject Nannie's tragic vision and commit herself to the world around her and deal with it more effectively than Nannie.

It is necessary to mention these differences because they help define the strengths and weaknesses of the play. When Nannie takes over and we see everything in relation to her, O'Casey communicates a powerful vision of a deranged world, a vision which a short play could sustain. But when the widow takes over, we see the engaging contrast between the earthy realism and common sense of the widow, tempered somewhat by her love of malapropism, and the folly and vanity of the suitors who are in their second childhood but won't admit it. The trouble is that these two perspectives relate to ultimately different experiences, each of which distracts attention from the other. As a result, though striking and amusing, the play is uneven.

The next two plays, *The End of the Beginning* and *A Pound on Demand,* written apparently in the early 1930's, are generally farcical. They concentrate on essentially trivial everyday events in which the irrational seems to be an intrusion into an ordered, reasonable world. However, this ordered world also turns out to have its own illogic, if only because its characters are so forcefully endowed with stupidity. In both plays O'Casey sustains this interplay between the irrational and the supposedly rational ingeniously.

The End of the Beginning concerns a stupid, boastful, lazy, and domineering husband who wants to put his wife in her place by daring her that he can do her work better than she. This kind of nonsense, which has a definite limit so far as development is concerned, is appropriate for a one act. If carried too far, clearly the situation loses its absurdity and can become boring. The obvious irrationality is the husband's uncontrollable vanity and wish for domination. This causes him first of all to make such a fiasco of the whole effort by browbeating a dimwitted, incredibly near-sighted friend into doing most of the chores. Because of the latter's physical handicaps, he virtually wrecks the house. The friend's vanity also contributes because he insists upon showing off his prowess. The less obvious, yet equally important irrationality, is the wife's so-called common sense, which really masks her vanity. She thinks she can cure her husband of his folly by playing along with him. She doesn't realise that the husband (like Captain Boyle in *Juno*), makes up the rules and that in wanting to humiliate her husband she is only indulging her own vanity. In the end, the husband, like Boyle, simply projects the blame onto her so that he actually has won. He is undaunted as ever while she has to repair the damage she helped cause.

In this play the irrational represents childish indulgence of one's whims. And the play shows us what fine, destructive momentum such indulgence can create, par-

204

ticularly among the stupid whom it exhilarates. The same is true in *A Pound on Demand* where the trivial action is a drunk's attempt, aided by a wheedling friend, to match his signature so as to draw money from his savings account. O'Casey cuts the action off just when it could seem almost inexhaustible. Presented as it is, such action brings about a kind of recklessness that for a short time is destructive and outrageous. But only for a short period.

The next group of plays—*Time to Go, Hall of Healing,* and *Bedtime Story*—all presumably written about the same time and published and produced in 1951, significantly resemble the four preceding plays. *Bedtime Story* concerns itself with the irrationality of every day life, as it amusingly explores the relation between propriety and sexuality. The other two plays critically portray more serious folly and injustices in Irish community and institutional life.

Time to Go reminds us of *Kathleen* because it seems superficial and stilted, though possibly for different reasons. It portrays a different Ireland than that of the last plays, a country where the alliance between the Church and prominent business leaders has impaired, if not denied, true Christianity. Through the varied business activities of people at a county fair, O'Casey contrasts for us two kinds of commitment, the simple human kindness that is authentically Christian in the spirit of the saints, and the pietistic Christianity which the business men use to rationalise their money making and their greed. Formally, the play combines satiric realism in the portrayal of the business men and fantasy in the portrayal of the authentic Christians, a naive and simple man and a woman, who, however, turn out to be saints, or near equivalents. The blatant contradiction between spurious and authentic Christianity provides the basis here for the irrational, or the obviously illogical. But the play doesn't explore this contradiction interestingly enough because the characters on both levels seem like crude stereotypes. The business men say all the right things to characterise their position but display almost no feeling, or that of the most obvious sort, and the two local saints seem pallid and uninteresting. As a result, the contradiction that O'Casey wishes to dramatise loses much of its force.

Much more serious in implication and yet much more lighthearted in a grotesque way than *Time to Go* is *Hall of Healing*. The play depicts the treatment of the Dublin poor in a public medical dispensary during a typical day. While *Hall of Healing* is based on O'Casey's memory of his own visits to such a dispensary in his youth, it is universal because it portrays resignation as a terrible, complex condition of life that affects all concerned, even the doctor. As one character bitterly remarks, all the people in the dispensary are in a dance of death. However, they don't know it and they blindly remain alive. The dance motif is evident by the emphasis on movement. Each patient hops to his place in the line, and the attendant, called Allelulia, wildly dances when he hears music from an adjoining church.

In the play the irrational assumes a number of comic and serious meanings, though all of them are related, and each accentuates the other. We see the comic in the childish pleasure the characters derive from getting one colour medicine rather than another, in the absurd rule that each new patient bring three bottles (one for each basic kind of medicine he might get), the characters' proud boasts about their ailments, and Allelulia's insistence upon 'expostulating' with the patients, that is lecturing them and harassing them instead of helping them. On this plane the play is humorous because characters settle for minor pleasures or satisfactions or, conversely, minor outlets for frustration. But they do so because they are reduced by their environment to resignation, which is the only commitment they can make. There is the stoical resignation of an eighty-year-old woman who prefers to suffer in the cold rather than try to persuade the chief attendant to let her stand inside until the dispensary officially opens, the maniacal fear of the attendant to placate the doctor because subconsciously he himself feels so hopeless, and the bitter, half-destructive, half-intelligent resignation of the doctor himself trying to reconcile his hatred for his job and his patients with his intelligence that tells him he must do something, although it can't help much.

From one point of view, acceptance of resignation itself is irrational. That is, it is illogical and destructive, as one character called Red Muffler, who makes some effort to fight, points out, because it only perpetuates existing abuses. The more terrible truth the play reveals, however, is that all these people are too far gone to embrace any other attitude. For them to try to change would be more foolish because they lack the intelligence and the means, a fact which Red Muffler in his protest does not realise. The most they can do is try to understand and accept their common fate as suffering human beings. This is the only meaningful commitment open to them. Yet, even this barely seems within reach of any of the characters, except perhaps in a vague way when the old woman tries to console Red Muffler's wife for the loss of her child. Otherwise, the characters continue blindly and foolishly on. At the end Allelulia callously and meticulously closes up the dispensary and prepares for another day during which he can 'expostulate' but be driven by his absurd fears.

Bedtime Story reveals the frantic efforts of a fearful, proper, young bachelor to sneak out of his room a girl with whom he has had intercourse so that those who embody propriety for him—his landlady, fellow lodger, and parish priest—won't find him out. In this play, as in many of the other later ones, O'Casey exposes the absurdity of living by appearances and seeking rigorous external sanction for behavior rather than accepting one's impulses openly and honestly. Here the irrational takes two forms: a deliberate weapon the girl uses to revenge herself on the young man whom she comes to despise for his hypocrisy and fear of his way of life, and, on the other hand, the ultimate form that such a way of life assumes for those who, like the young man, let it govern them. Angela, the girl, frankly enjoys her sexual and sensual nature and doesn't worry about the neighbours or anyone else for that matter. John Jo Mulligan, in contrast, lives in mortal fear of jeopardising his reputation as a high-type, clean-cut young man. Having such a reputation makes John Jo feel that he doesn't have to accept responsibility for his impulses, particularly those of sex which scare him, because he lets people like his landlady be his conscience. Nevertheless, because he works so hard to keep up appearances, he thinks he has a right to indulge such impulses as sex. For John Jo, fear and self-interest have precariously stabilised themselves in a devotion to appearances.

Angela, however, threatens his equilibrium, and in doing so reveals another possibility which a one act can exploit, a sustained 'put on'. This is just what she is doing so well but only for a short time, for the play's strength depends on the fact that time is at a premium. Sooner or later John Jo must reach the breaking point.

First Angela teases him simply out of amusement and high spirits. But then, as indicated, out of disgust for his fear of exposure and his own self-righteousness, she begins to use hysterics, threats, pleas of injured innocence—the feigned irrational—to make as much noise as she can. Consequently, he is torn between his fear of being found out and his self-interest and smugness, which make him think he has a right to save his skin. At first, fear seems to win out. He lets Angela walk off with twenty-eight pounds to pay for a purse she claimed she lost in his flat, not to mention his umbrella, his coat, and a valuable diamond ring. But when he remembers that she had no purse in the first place, self-interest and revenge take over, and he gets caught in his own trap. When his landlady, who also accepts appearances as the ultimate reality, sees him running out into the street in his slippers, raving and shouting, she concludes that he must be mad, and tries to have him committed. Such an ending is ironically appropriate because the landlady and lodger do represent that very world which up to this point has given John Jo his precarious security. While such an ending may seem almost too neat, the rest of the play shows great comic invention. When John Jo, for example, is afraid to put on the light while Angela is dressing, she cleverly teases him : 'Switch on the light for God's sake, man, and let's have a look at each other before you banish your poor Eve from her Mulligan paradise.'

As O'Casey's last one-act play, *The Moon Shines on Kylenamoe* seems appropriate because it combines the two main tendencies of the irrational I have been describing—that of the trivial and personal, and that of the more serious and impersonal, and attempts to synthesise them.

The basic plot action certainly is trivial since it involves the incredibly difficult efforts of a British diplomatic functionary to get transportation from an obscure railroad station, at which he has alighted, to a nearby castle where, of all people, the British Prime Minister happens to be visiting. The play, however, has a more impersonal and larger frame of reference, for the Englishman keeps encountering representative Irishmen with an astonishing assortment of prejudices and irresponsible opinions. Such encounters dramatise the central subject of the play, the extraordinary difficulty people have in communicating, even in so simple a thing as renting a car. In such a context, the irrational becomes the prejudiced, the willful, the crotchety, the indulgence of feeling at the expense of fact or logic.

There is still another perspective in which the irrational assumes more value. In this perspective it seems to be a kind of defence against kindness and compassion, a way of masking a commitment until one feels safe to make a larger one. This is evident towards the very end of the play, when, after the train has pulled out, the Englishman seems stranded, an old railroad labourer (who lives near the station) offers him hospitality. Although the offer is genuine, the labourer is prepared to be hostile because he will not risk being rejected or being embarrassed. As a result, he spars gingerly with the Englishman until he can let down his guard. Then all parties involved, the labourer, his wife, and the Englishman suddenly act differently and throw away their masks. When it is now clear that the labourer will not be embarrassed because of showing kindness, his wife comes forward and warmly welcomes the Englishman. In turn, the Englishman thanks her because he knows how difficult an ordeal she and her husband have gone through. I don't mean to imply that this episode is so complex and subtle, but only how delicate and real are the characters' feelings and how intuitively they understand and respect one another. In part, the characters can do so because they have taken such pains with their feelings. They even indulge their prejudices, their fears, and their absurd suspicions. But by the same token, most of the time they simply weren't communicating their deepest feelings because they were all acting illogically and capriciously.

In short, O'Casey explores each manifestation of the irrational and its implications in its own terms and degree of importance. This means both recognising what is really serious, at the same time paying loving, but strict, tribute to the trivial. As Eric Bentley tells us in his discussion of Wilde's *The Importance of Being Earnest*,[62] this is a sign of being truly civilised. This very precision, moreover, helps us understand some of the best and worst features of the longer plays. In the one acts, O'Casey has a fine talent for isolating a particular manifestation of the irrational and presenting it as a distinct impression, complete to itself. In his very best longer plays, he manages to include a much greater range of such impressions as part of a dynamically unified larger experience. However, in some of his more uneven plays, such as *Within the Gates* and *The Bishop's Bonfire,* the impressions are fleeting and contradictory, and almost detached from the rest of the play.

FOOTNOTES

1. David Krause, *Sean O'Casey, The Man and His Work* (New York: Macmillan, 1960); Robert Hogan, *The Experiments of Sean O'Casey* (New York: St. Martin's Press, 1960); Ronald Ayling, ed., *Sean O'Casey: Modern Judgements* (London: Macmillan, 1969).

2. Roy Harvey Pearce, 'The Poet as Person,' *Interpretations of American Literature*, ed. Charles Feidelson and Paul Brodkorb (New York: Oxford, 1960) p. 370.

3. Krause, 'Sean O'Casey: 1880–1964,' *The Massachusetts Review*, vol. VI (Spring, 1965) p. 240.

4. Sean O'Casey, 'Holographic Notebooks,' vol. 13, p. 43 (unpublished manuscript in the Berg Collection, New York Public Library).

5. Lady Isabella Augusta Gregory, *Lady Gregory's Journals*, ed. Lennox Robinson (London: Putnam, 1946) p. 75.

6. Anthony Butler in 'The Early Background,' in *The World of Sean O'Casey*, ed. Sean McCann (London: Four Square Press, 1966) p. 16, points out that the house in which O'Casey was born was *not* in the slums. I also understand from Countess Karin von der Schulenberg, former Editor of the Mercier Press, that Evelyn Jansson in an M.A. thesis, *The Early Years of Sean O'Casey*, (University College Dublin) sets out to prove that O'Casey did not live in a slum. However, I have not seen Miss Jansson's thesis. Yet granting that Butler may be right, it is undeniable that O'Casey *did* live in the slums for a significant portion of his life.

7. Krause, *Sean O'Casey: The Man and His Work, op. cit.*, p. 4.

8. Krause, 'Sean O'Casey: 1880–1964,' *op. cit.*, p. 240.

9. Jack Lindsay, 'Sean O'Casey as a Socialist Artist.' Ronald Ayling, ed., *Sean O'Casey: Modern Judgements, op. cit.*, p. 190.

10. Hogan, ed., *Feathers from the Green Crow; Sean O'Casey, 1905–1925* (Columbia: University of Missouri, 1962) p. 183.

11. Lady Gregory, *op. cit.*, p. 260.

12. Quoted in Lindsay, 'Sean O'Casey as a Socialist Artist,' in *Sean O'Casey*, Ayling, ed., *op. cit.*, p. 194.

13. O'Casey dedicated Volume III of his autobiography, *Innishfallen Fare Thee Well*, to Dr. McDonald. The dedication reveals O'Casey's feelings: 'A Great Man Gone, and Almost Forgotten; but Not Quite Forgotten.'

14. Desmond Ryan, *Remembering Sion* (London: Arthur Baker, 1934), quoted in Hogan, ed., *Feathers from the Green Crow: Sean O'Casey, 1905–1925, op. cit.*, xi.

15. William Armstrong, 'History, Biography, and *The Shadow of a Gunman*,' *Modern Drama*, vol. III (1960) p. 418.

16. *Ibid.*, p. 421.

17. All quotations from the plays are from the English edition published by Macmillan, London. Except for *The Bishop's*

Bonfire (1955) and *The Drums of Father Ned* (1960), the others are in *Collected Plays*, Vols. I, II (1949); Vols. III, IV (1951).

Juno and the Paycock

18. *Cf.* Dorothy MacArdle, *The Irish Republic* (Dublin: Irish Press, 1951) p. 251ff.

19. *Ibid.*, p. 279.

20. O'Casey, *Innishfallen Fare Thee Well*, in *Autobiographies*, vol. II (London: Macmillan, 1963) p. 91.

21. Gabriel Fallon, *Sean O'Casey: The Man I Knew* (London: Routledge and Kegan Paul, 1965) p. 24.

The Plough and the Stars

22. For a view of Easter, 1916, that in many respects corresponds to O'Casey's, cf. the play of Conor Cruise O'Brien, 'Embers of Easter,' in *1916, The Easter Rising*, ed. O. Dudley Edwards and Fergus Pyle (London: Macgibbon & Kee, 1968) pp. 223–241.

23. Tim Pat Coogan, 'The Exile,' in Sean McCann, ed., *The World of Sean O'Casey*, *op. cit.*, p. 115.

24. William Armstrong, 'The Sources and Themes of *The Plough and the Stars*,' *Modern Drama*, vol. IV (December, 1961), p. 235.

25. *Ibid.*

26. O'Casey, *Drums Under the Window*, in *Autobiographies*, vol. I, *op. cit.*, p. 684.

27. Hogan, *The Experiments of Sean O'Casey*, *op. cit.*, pp. 41–54.

28. *Ibid.*, p. 45.

Introduction: Towards a New Jerusalem

29. O'Casey, *Rose and Crown* in *Autobiographies*, vol. II, *op. cit.*, pp. 313–321.

30. A reading of Mrs. O'Casey's book certainly strengthens our impressions of the dire financial straits in which the O'Casey's lived and their rich and warm family and personal life. Only in the last two years of O'Casey's life did the family have any real economic security; all the rest of the time Mrs. O'Casey had to use her wits, her endurance, and her charm to avert disaster. From Mrs. O'Casey's descriptions of family life, it is clear how lively, affectionate, and generally serene that life was. But what is also evident is how much the O'Casey's needed and valued each other. Mrs. O'Casey fulfilled herself through her family and husband. In doing so, she subordinated her career to his and assumed a great many of the family responsibilities. As a result, O'Casey, despite all the economic stress, remained free to devote himself wholly to his writing—and on his terms. Yet Mrs. O'Casey did far more than merely enable O'Casey to go on with

his writing. She was the vital center of his life, the source of his deepest and richest personal happiness. Her presence made wherever she was home for O'Casey; her absence (as he reveals in this letter written on the first occasion when they were separated for more than a day or so) made him always unbearably lonely:

> The first time since we came together that you have been away from me for some days, and my heart, darling and beautiful Eily, is heavier than I wished to be. Curious quietness about the house today and now tonight quieter still—quiet and not a little sad. Strange sense of calm restlessness, not of the body but of the spirit—yes, of the body too, really; a curiously quiet, uneasy restlessness that nothing will remove but the clasping in my arms again of my darling Eileen. I look at the things in your room and in my room, and they, too, seem to have gathered into them some of the patient resentment of your absence.
>
> I miss you, Eily; I miss you very much indeed. Your going away has shaken an uneasy silence over everything that I see, and everything that I touch. Everything is the same, yet nothing is as it was. Eileen Carey—beautiful, brown-haired, white-breasted Eileen Carey is very, very, very dear to Sean (*Sean*, p. 191).

Mrs. O'Casey, for her part, reveals now much she cares in two ways. One is by the sheer concentration on the details of the shared O'Casey life. The second, and it comes only at the very end after O'Casey's death, expresses her loneliness and need:

> Here, then, I am; I can travel; I can go where I like when I wish. But when Sean was alive it was possible to go out with the knowledge that he would be at home waiting for me; now nobody, when I return, will listen to all I have done, share my moods of happiness or depression. I have had to adjust myself to a life without Sean; without having him to look after; without him to look after me; without our talk and our jokes; without anyone to admire me as he did; without anybody to whom I belong.
>
> I dread the stillness I walk into; the solitude. Deeply now, and always, I miss opening the door and not hearing Sean's voice, warm and welcoming: 'Is that you, Eileen?' (*Sean*, *Ibid.*, p. 300).

The Silver Tassie

31. For detailed discussion of the controversy cf. Krause, 'The Playwright's Not for Burning,' *The Virginia Quarterly Review*, vol. 34 (Winter, 1958) pp. 60–76. Also cf. Hogan, *The Experiments of*

Sean O'Casey, *op. cit.*, pp. 184–206, and *The Letters of W. B. Yeats*, ed. Allan Wade (New York: Macmillan, 1954) pp. 740–742.

32. In particular see Irving Wardle's discussion of the play in *The London Times*, 11 Sept. and 13 Sept. 1969, and Philip Hope Wallace in *The Guardian*, 11 Sept. 1969.

33. I want to express my thanks to the Director of the play, Mr. David Jones, for this courtesy.

34. C. R. M. F. Cruttwell, *A History of the Great War: 1914–1918* (Oxford: Clarendon Press, 1934) p. 325.

35. *Ibid.*, p. 382.

36. Ronald Bryden, 'O'Casey and His Raw Torso,' *The Observer*, (14 September 1969) p. 26.

37. O'Casey, *The Silver Tassie* (typescript copy, Berg Collection, New York Public Library) [revised and corrected for publication.]

Within the Gates

38. O'Casey, *Rose and Crown*, in *Autobiographies*, vol. II *op. cit.*, p. 352.

39. John Raymond, ed., *The Baldwin Age* (London: Eyre & Spottiswoode, 1960) p. 138.

40. Cf. Stark Young's review in 'Theatre,' *The New Republic*, vol. LXXX (7 November 1934) p. 369.

Purple Dust

41. Krause, *Sean O'Casey: The Man and His Work*, *op. cit.*, p. 186.

The Star Turns Red

42. Pat Esslinger, 'Sean O'Casey and the Lockout of 1913, *Materia Poetica* of Two Red Plays,' *Modern Drama*, vol. VI (May, 1963) pp. 55–57.

43. Emmett Larkin, *James Larkin, Labour Leader* (London: Routledge and Kegan Paul, 1965) p. 121.

44. Esslinger, *op. cit.*, p. 59.

Oak Leaves and Lavender

45. Krause, *Sean O'Casey: The Man and His Work*, *op. cit.*, p. 161.

46. Harold Clurman in his review of the play, *The Nation*, vol. CLXXXII (14 January 1956) p. 39.

47. O'Casey, *Innishfallen Fare Thee Well*, in *Autobiographies*, vol. II, *op. cit.*, pp. 186–199.

Introduction: Ireland Revisited

48. Cf. Hogan, 'O'Casey and the Archbishop,' *The New Republic*, vol. CXXXVIII (19 May 1958) pp. 29–30.

49. Coogan, 'The Exile,' in *The World of Sean O'Casey*, ed. Sean McCann, *op. cit.*, p. 126.

50. Niall Carroll, 'The Bonfire,' in *Ibid.* p. 133. Alec Reid in 'The Legend of the Green Crow,' *Drama Survey*, vol. III (Spring-Summer, 1963) pp. 155–163, also defends the Tosthal authorities.

51. John Gassner, 'The Prodigality of Sean O'Casey,' *Theatre Arts*, vol. 35 (June, 1951) p. 53.

52. Catherine Ryne, 'O'Casey in His Letters,' in *The World of Sean O'Casey*, ed. McCann, *op. cit.*, p. 240.

53. O'Brien, 'The Embers of Easter,' in O. Dudley Edwards and Fergus Pyle, eds. *1916, The Easter Rising, op. cit.*, p. 238.

The Bishop's Bonfire

54.   In order to arrive there,
   To arrive where you are, to get from where you are not,
   You must go by a way wherein there is no ecstasy
   In order to arrive at what you do not know.
   You must go by a way which is the way of ignorance.
   T. S. Eliot, 'East Coker,' Section III, in *The Complete Poems and Plays 1900–1950* (New York: Harcourt, Brace and World, 1962) p. 127.

55. Edna O'Brien, *Encore*, vol. VI (September-October, 1961) p. 42.

The Drums of Father Ned

56. G. Wilson Knight, *The Christian Renaissance* (New York: W. W. Norton, 1962) pp. 345–346.

57. *Ibid.*, p. 346.

Conclusion

58. Coogan, 'The Exile,' in *The World of Sean O'Casey*, ed. McCann, *op. cit.*, p. 127. Also cf. Michael Sheehy, *Is Ireland Dying?* (New York: Taplinger, 1969), especially pp. 103–157, which substantiates many of these same ideas.

59. Krause, 'Sean O'Casey: 1880–1964,' *op. cit.*, p. 252.

60. Hogan, ed., *Feathers from the Green Crow, op. cit.*, xiii.

Appendix; The One Act Plays

61. 'Kathleen Listens In' and 'Nannie's Night Out' can be found in *Feathers from the Green Crow*, Hogan, ed., *op. cit.*, pp. 267–336. There is also a version of 'Nannie's Night Out' in the Berg Collection at the New York Public Library [but I have not as yet been able to examine it.]

62. Eric Bentley, ed., *The Play* (New York: Prentice Hall, 1951) p. 287.

BIBLIOGRAPHY

I. By Sean O'Casey

Autobiography, London; Macmillan, 1963, 2 vols. See notation for American edition, *Mirror in My House*.

The Bishop's Bonfire. London: Macmillan, 1955.

Blasts and Benedictions. New York: St. Martins, 1967.

'Cat 'n' Cage,' vol. 16, *The Virginia Quarterly Review* (July 1940) pp. 425–445.

Collected Plays (London: Macmillan), 4 vols.

> Vol. I (1949) *Juno and the Paycock; The Shadow of a Gunman; The Plough and the Stars; The End of the Beginning; A Pound on Demand.*

> Vol. II (1949) *The Silver Tassie; Within the Gates; The Star Turns Red.*

> Vol. III (1951) *Purple Dust; Red Roses for Me; Hall of Healing.*

> Vol. IV (1951) *Oak Leaves and Lavender; Cock-a-Doodle Dandy; Bedtime Story; Time to Go.*

'Daily Worker,' vol. 22, *New Statesman and Nation* (7 Aug. 1941) p. 111.

'The Delicate Art of Growing Old,' vol. 219, *Harpers* (Aug. 1959) pp. 65–66.

'The Dream School,' vol. XXVI, *The Yale Review* (Summer 1937) pp. 718–723.

The Drums of Father Ned, London: Macmillan, 1960.

Feathers from the Green Crow: Sean O'Casey 1905–1925, ed. Robert Hogan, Columbia: University of Missouri, 1962).

The Flying Wasp, New York: Macmillan, 1937.

The Green Crow, New York: George Braziller, 1957.

'The Harp in the Air Still Sings,' *The New York Times Magazine* (11 Jan 1959), VI, p. 11.

'I Predict,' vol. 26, *Look* (16 Jan. 1962) p. 18.

'Jeeps, Be Jeepers,' vol. 46, *The New Statesman and Nation* (18 July 1953) p. 70.

'Irish Childhood,' vol. 356, *The Living Age* (June 1939) pp. 391–394.

'Letter to Mr. Ryan,' vol. 44, *Theatre Arts* (Feb. 1960) pp. 21–22.

'Out Damned Spot,' vol. 44, *Theatre Arts* (May 1960) pp. 21–22.

Mirror in My House, New York: Macmillan, 1956; 2 Vols.

> Vol. I *I Knock at the Door, Pictures in the Hallway, Drums Under the Window.*

> Vol. II *Innishfallen Fare Thee Well, Rose and Crown, Sunset and Evening Star.*

'Play of Ideas,' vol. 39, *New Statesman and Nation* (8 April 1950) pp. 397–398.

'Plays of Sean O'Casey,' vol. 104, *Nineteenth Century* (Sept. 1928) pp. 399–402.

'Royal Residence,' vol. 16, *The Virginia Quarterly Review* (Jan. 1940) pp. 51–67.

'Saintly Sinner, Sing for Us,' vol. 40, *New Statesman and Nation* (16 Dec. 1950) p. 628.

'St. Pathrick's Day in the Morning,' *New York Times Magazine* (15 March 1953) p. 17.

'Sean O'Casey Concerning James Joyce,' vol. V, *The Massachusetts Review* (Spring 1964) pp. 335–336.

Selected Plays, ed. John Gassner, New York: George Braziller, 1956.

The Story of the Irish Citizen Army, Dublin: Maunsel, 1919.

Three Plays : Behind the Green Curtains, Figuro in the Night, and *The Moon Shines on Kylenamoe*, New York: St. Martins, 1961.

Under a Colored Cap, London: Macmillan, 1963.

II. About Sean O'Casey and His World

Adams, Phoebe, 'The Reader's Choice,' vol. 196, *The Atlantic Monthly* (October 1955) pp. 88–97. (Discussion of *The Bishop's Bonfire*.)

Agate, James, *First Nights*, London: Nicholson and Watson, 1934.

———: *James Agate: An Anthology*, ed. Herbert Van Thal, London: Hart-Davis, 1961.

Aickman, R. F., 'Mr. Sean O'Casey and the Striker,' vol. 139, *Nineteenth Century* (April 1946) pp. 172–175.

Armstrong, William A., 'History, Biography, and *The Shadow of a Gunman*,' vol. III, *Modern Drama* (September 1960) pp. 417–424.

———: 'The Irish Point of View,' The Plays of Sean O'Casey, Brendan Behan, and Thomas Murphy, vol. 14, *Experimental Drama* (Winter 1964) pp. 79–102.

———: *Sean O'Casey*, London: Longmans, Green, 1967.

———: 'The Sources and Themes of *The Plough and the Stars*,' vol. IV, *Modern Drama* (December 1961) pp. 230–250.

Ayling, Ronald, 'Sean O'Casey: Fact and Fancy,' vol. VII, *The Massachusetts Review* (1966) pp. 603–612.

———: 'Feathers Finely Aflutter,' vol. VII, *Modern Drama* (Sept. 1964) pp. 135–147.

———: 'Nannie's Night Out,' vol. V, *Modern Drama* (May 1962) pp. 154–163.

———: ed. *Sean O'Casey: Modern Judgments*, London: Macmillan, 1969.

Baggett, Patricia, 'Sean O'Casey's Development of a Basic Theme,' vol. XXXI, *Dublin Magazine* (IV, 1956) pp. 25–34.

Barnes, Clive, 'Review of *Cock-a-Doodle Dandy*,' *New York Times*, 21 January 1969, p. 40.

Barry, Tom B., *Guerrilla Days in Ireland*, New York: Devin Adair, 1956.

Behan, Brendan, *Borstal Boy*, New York: Alfred A. Knopf, 1959.

———: *The Hostage*, New York: Grove, 1958.

———: *The Quare Fellow*, New York: Grove, 1956.

218

——: *The Scarperer*, New York: Doubleday, 1964.

Bennett, Richard, *The Black and Tans*, London: Hullin, 1959.

Bentley, Eric, 'The Case of O'Casey,' vol. CXXVII, *The New Republic* (13 Oct. 1952) p. 17.

——: *The Dramatic Event*, New York: Horizon Press, 1954.

——: *In Search of Theatre*, New York: Alfred A. Knopf, 1953.

——: *The Life of the Drama*, New York: Athenaeum, 1964.

——: *The Playwright as Thinker*, New York: Reynal and Hitchcock, 1946.

——: 'Theatre,' vol. CXXXIV, *The New Republic* (30 Jan. 1956) p. 21.

——: *What is Theatre*, New York: Horizon Press, 1956.

Bergholz, H., 'Sean O'Casey,' vol. 65, *English Studies* (1 Nov. 1930) pp. 49–67.

Boyd, Ernest, 'Sean O'Casey; Still Knocking at the Door,' vol. 25, *Saturday Review of Literature* (21 March 1942) p. 5.

Boucicault, Dion, *The Dolmen Boucicault*, ed. David Krause, Dublin: Dolmen Press, 1964.

——: *The Shaughraun*, London: Samuel French, 1875.

Brown, J., 'Juno and the Paycock,' vol. 140, *The Saturday Review* (21 Nov. 1925) p. 594.

——: 'The Silver Tassie,' vol. 145, *The Saturday Review* (23 June 1928) pp. 801–802.

——: 'The Silver Tassie,' vol. 148, *The Saturday Review* (19 Oct. 1929) p. 446.

Bryden, Ronald, 'O'Casey and His Raw Torso,' *The Observer*, 14 September 1969, p. 26.

Byrne, Dawson, *The Story of Ireland's National Theatre*, Dublin: The Talbot Press, 1929.

Carroll, J., 'O'Casey the Emigrant Titan,' vol. 36, *Theatre Arts* (Dec. 1952) pp. 6–8.

Carroll, Paul Vincent, *Irish Stories and Plays*, New York: Devin Adair, 1959.

——: *Shadow and Substance*, New York: Random House, 1937.

——: *Things That Are Caesars*, London: Rich & Cowan, 1934.

——: *The Wayward Saint*, New York: Dramatists Play Service, 1955.

——: *The White Steed and Coggerers*, New York: Random House, 1939.

Caulfield, Malachy Francis, *The Easter Rebellion*, New York: Holt, Rinehart, Winston, 1963.

Clurman, Harold, 'Bard in a Pub,' vol. CLXXIX, *The Nation* (27 Nov. 1954) p. 468.

——: 'Theatre,' vol. CLXXXVII, *The Nation* (29 Nov. 1958) p. 416. (Review of *The Plough and the Stars*.)

——: 'Theatre,' vol. CXLI, *The Nation* (24 Dec. 1960) p. 510. (Review of *The Plough and the Stars*.)

——: 'Theatre: Off Broadway,' vol. CXXI, *The New Republic* (19 Sept. 1949) p. 21. (Review of *The Silver Tassie*.)

——: 'Theatre,' vol. CLXXXII, *The Nation* (14 Jan 1956) pp. 39–40. (Review of *Red Roses for Me*.)

Codman, F., 'Sean O'Casey,' vol. CXXXVIII, *The Nation* (25 April 1934) pp. 476–477.

Colum, Padraic, 'Sean O'Casey,' vol. 9, *Theatre Arts Monthly* (June 1925) pp. 396–404.

——: 'Wallops in Autobiography,' vol. CXXXI, *The New Republic* (27 Dec. 1954) p. 19.

Connolly, T. L., 'The Case of Sean O'Casey: Reply,' vol. 23, *Commonweal* (14 Feb. 1936) p. 442.

Corkery, Daniel, *Synge and Anglo Irish Literature*, Dublin and Cork: Cork University Press, 1931.

Coston, Herbert, 'The Idea of Courage in O'Casey's Plays,' Unpublished Ph.D. Thesis, Columbia University, 1961.

Cruttwell, C. R. M. F., *A History of the Great War, 1914–1918*, Oxford: Clarendon Press, 1934.

Edwards, O. Dudley and Pyle, Fergus, ed., *1916, The Easter Rising*, London: MacGibbon and Kee, 1968.

Edwards, Dudley, ed., *Conor Cruise O'Brien Introduces Ireland*, London: Andre Deutsch, 1969.

Esslinger, Pat, 'Sean O'Casey and the Lockout of 1913: *Materia Poetica* of Two Red Plays,' vol. VI, *Modern Drama*, May 1963, pp. 55–57.

Fallon, Gabriel, 'Pathway of a Dramatist,' vol. 34, *Theatre Arts*, (January 1950) pp. 336–339.

——: *'Sean O'Casey: The Man I Knew*,' London: Routledge and Kegan Paul, 1965.

Fay, Gerard, *The Abbey Theatre*, London: Hollis & Carter, 1958.

Fox, Richard Michael, *Green Banners*, London: Secker and Warburg, 1938.

——: *The History of the Irish Citizen Army*, Dublin: J. Duffy, 1943.

——: *Jim Larkin*, London: Laurence and Wishart, 1957.

——: 'Sean O'Casey: A Worker Dramatist,' vol. 26, *The New Statesman* (10 April 1926) pp. 805–806.

F. R. B., 'Lights Down,' vol. 148, *The Outlook* (1 February 1928) p. 187. (Review of *The Plough and the Stars*.)

Freedman, Morris, 'The Modern Tragicomedy of Wilde and O'Casey,' vol. XXV, *College English* (April 1964) pp. 518–527.

Gascoigne, Bamber, 'The Symbol on the Carpet,' vol. 207, *Spectator* (11 August 1961) p. 204. (Review of *The Bishop's Bonfire*.)

Gassner, John, 'The Prodigality of Sean O'Casey,' vol. 35, *Theatre Arts* (June 1951) pp. 52–53; vol. 35 (July 1951) pp. 54–55; vol. 35 (August 1951), pp. 48–49.

Gilder, Rosamond, 'Broadway in Review,' vol. 24, *Theatre Arts Monthly* (March 1940) p. 162. (Review of *Juno and the Paycock*.)

220

Gellert, Roger, 'Wring Its Neck,' vol. 62, *The New Statesman and Nation* (4 August 1961) p. 164. (Review of *The Bishop's Bonfire*.)

Goldstone, Herbert, 'The Unevenness of O'Casey's *Within the Gates*,' Forum, University of Houston (Spring 1965) pp. 89–102.

Greene, David H., 'Great Dramatists' Approach to Autobiography,' vol. 65, *Commonweal* (25 January 1957) pp. 440–443.

Gregory, Augusta, *Lady Gregory's Journals*, ed. Lennox Robinson, London: Putnam and Company, 1946.

——: *Selected Plays*, London: Putnam and Company, 1962.

Gregory, Horace, 'Playwright on a Soapbox,' vol. 37, *Saturday Review of Literature* (20 Nov. 1954) p. 18.

Hatch, Robert, 'Theatre and Films,' vol. CLXXXIV, *The Nation* (19 Jan. 1957) p. 65. (Review of *Purple Dust*.)

Hethomon, Robert, 'Great Hatred, Little Room,' vol. IV, *The Tulane Drama Review* (Summer 1961) pp. 51–55.

Hewes, Henry, 'Broadway Postscript,' vol. 38, *The Saturday Review of Literature* (19 Nov. 1955) p. 37. (Review of *Cock-a-Doodle Dandy*.)

——: 'Broadway Postscript,' vol. 42, *The Saturday Review of Literature* (9 May 1959) p. 22. (Review of *The Drums of Father Ned*.)

——: 'Broadway Postscript,' vol. 36, *The Saturday Review of Literature* (6 June 1953) pp. 24–25. (Review of *The Plough and the Stars*.)

——: 'Broadway Postscript,' vol. 40, *The Saturday Review of Literature* (19 Jan. 1957) p. 48. (Review of *Purple Dust*.)

Hogan, Robert, *After the Irish Renaissance*, Minneapolis: University of Minnesota Press, 1967.

——: *The Experiments of Sean O'Casey*, New York: St. Martins, 1960.

——: 'O'Casey and the Archbishop,' vol. CXXXVIII, *The New Republic* (19 May 1958) pp. 29–30.

——: 'O'Casey's Dramatic Apprenticeship,' vol. IV, *Modern Drama* (Summer 1961) pp. 243–253.

——: 'Reply to Vivian Mercier.' vol. 64, *Commonweal* (24 Aug. 1956) p. 517.

Holt, Edgar, *Protest in Arms: The Irish Troubles, 1916–23*, London: Putnam and Company, 1960.

Hone, Joseph, *W. B. Yeats*, London: Macmillan, 1942.

Igoe, W. J., 'Literature and the Arts,' vol. 91, *America* (14 Aug. 1954) p. 481. (Review of *The Plough and the Stars*.)

Issacs, Edith J. R., 'Playhouse Gates,' vol. 18, *Theatre Arts Monthly* (Dec. 1934) pp. 894–904. (Review of *Within the Gates*.)

Jennings, R., 'The Silver Tassie.' vol. 143, *The Spectator* (19 Oct. 1929) p. 523. (Review of *The Silver Tassie*.)

Johnston, Denis, *Collected Plays*, London: Jonathan Cape, 1960, 2 vols.

——: *The Golden Cockoo and Other Plays*, London: Jonathan Cape, 1954.

——: 'Sean O'Casey,' vol. CXCIX, *The New Republic* (3 Oct. 1964) p. 6.

——: 'Sean O'Casey, An Appreciation,' vol. 329, *The Living Age* (17 April 1926) pp. 161–163.

——: 'Sean O'Casey: A Biography and an Appraisal,' vol. IV, *Modern Drama* (Summer 1961) pp. 324–328.

Kavanagh, Peter, *The Story of the Abbey Theatre*, New York: Devin Adair, 1950.

Kelleher, J. N., 'O'Casey in Boston,' vol. CX, *The New Republic* (20 March 1944) p. 380.

Kerr, Walter, 'Review of *Cock-a-Doodle Dandy*, *New York Times*, 2 February 1969, II, p. 1. For replies cf. 2 March 1969, II, p. 15.

Knight, G. Wilson, *The Christian Renaissance*, New York: W. W. Norton, 1962.

Koslow, Jules, *The Red and the Green*, New York: 1958 (revised 1967).

Kowasjee, Saros, *Sean O'Casey: The Man Behind the Mask*, New York: St. Martins, 1964.

Krause, David, 'Sean O'Casey: 1880–1964,' vol. VI, *Massachusetts Review* (Winter-Spring 1965) pp. 233–252.

——: *Sean O'Casey: The Man and his Work* New York: Macmillan, 1960.

——: 'The Playwright's Not for Burning,' vol. 34, *The Virginia Quarterly Review* (Winter 1958) pp. 60–76.

——: 'The Rageous Ossean: Patron-Hero of Synge and O'Casey,' vol. IV, *Modern Drama* (Summer 1961) pp. 268–291.

Krutch, Joseph Wood, 'Drama: A Dublin Success,' vol. CXXII, *The Nation* (31 March 1926) p. 348. (Review of *Juno and the Paycock*.)

——: 'Mr. O'Casey's Charade,' vol. CXXXIX, *The Nation* (7 Nov. 1934) p. 546. (Review of *Within the Gates*.)

——: 'Poet Laureate,' vol. LXXV, *The Nation* (21 Dec. 1927) p. 718.

Lange, Victor, 'Review of *Felix Krull*,' vol. CXXXIII, *The New Republic* (3 Oct. 1955) pp. 19–21.

Larkin, Emmet, *James Larkin, Irish Labour Leader*, London: Routledge & Kegan Paul, 1965.

Lennon, M. J., 'Sean O'Casey and his Plays,' vol. 130, *Catholic World* (Dec. 1929) pp. 334–335.

Lewis, Allan, 'Sean O'Casey's World,' vol. CLXXXI, *The Nation* (24 Dec. 1955) pp. 555–556. (Review of *Red Roses for Me*.)

Lewis, Theophilus, 'Theatre,' vol. 94, *America* (21 Jan. 1956) pp. 459–460. (Review of *Red Roses for Me*.)

——: 'Theatre,' '*The Shadow of a Gunman*,' vol. 100, *America* (20 Dec. 1958) p. 382.

'Life, Letters, and the Arts,' vol. 321, *The Living Age* (3 May 1924) pp. 869–870. (Review of *Juno and the Paycock*.)

——: vol. 328, *The Living Age* (27 March 1926) pp. 693–694. (Review of *The Plough and the Stars*.)

222

Littlewood, S. R., '*The Plough and the Stars*.' vol. 70, *Bookman* (London) (May 1926) p. 130.

MacArdle, Dorothy, *The Irish Republic*, 4th ed., Dublin: Irish Press, 1951.

McCann, Sean, ed., *The World of Sean O'Casey*, London: Four Square Press, 1966.

MacCarthy, Desmond, *Drama*, London: Putnam and Company, 1940.

——: '*Juno and the Paycock*,' vol. 26, *The New Statesman and Nation* (28 Nov. 1925) p. 207.

——: '*The Plough and the Stars*,' vol. 27, *The New Statesman and Nation* (29 May 1926) p. 170.

——: *Theatre*, London: MacGibbon and Kee, 1954.

McDonald, Walter, *Reminiscences of a Maynooth Professor*, ed. Denis Gwynn, London, Jonathan Cape, 1925.

MacDonell, A. G., '*The Silver Tassie*,' vol. 21, *London Mercury* (Dec. 1929) pp. 166–167.

McHugh, Roger, ed., *Dublin 1916*, London: Arlington, 1966.

——: 'The Legacy of Sean O'Casey,' vol. VIII, *Texas Quarterly* (1965) pp. 123–137.

McLaughlin, J., 'Tired-out Oul' Blatherer,' vol. 100, *America* (7 March 1959) pp. 653–655.

Malcolm, Donald, 'Off Broadway: Import News,' vol. 34, *The New Yorker* (22 Nov. 1958) pp. 100–104. (Review of *Cock-a-Doodle Dandy*.)

Malone, A. E., 'Shadow of Sean O'Casey,' vol. 70, *Bookman* (London) (May 1926) pp. 104–107.

Malone, Maureen, *The Plays of Sean O'Casey*, Carbondale: Southern Illinois Press, 1970.

——: '*Red Roses for Me : Fact or Symbolism*,' vol. IX, *Modern Drama* (1966) pp. 147–152.

Martin, F. T., *Leaders and Men of the Irish Rising*, London: Methuen, 1967.

Mercier, Vivian, *The Irish Comic Tradition*, New York, Oxford, 1962.

——: 'The Riddle of Sean O'Casey,' vol. 64, *Commonweal* (13 July 1956) pp. 366–368. Correction: vol. 64 (21 Sept. 1956) p. 612.

Moses, Robert, 'Toast to O'Casey,' *New York Times Magazine* (1 Feb. 1959) p. 30.

Murray, Thomas C., *Aftermath*, Dublin: The Talbot Press, 1922.

——: *Birthright*, Dublin: Maunsel and Co., 1911.

——: *Maurice Harte and A Stag at Bay*, London: G. Allen and Unwin, 1934.

Nathan, George Jean, 'Best of the Irish,' vol. 15, *Newsweek* (29 Jan. 1940) p. 33.

——: *The World of George Jean Nathan*, ed. Charles Angoff, New York: Knopf, 1952.

O'Casey, Eileen, *Sean* (New York, Coward, McCann & Geoghagen, 1972).

O'Donnell, Donat, 'No Bishop, No Bonfire,' vol. 49, *The New Statesman and Nation* (5 March 1955) p. 320. (Review of *The Bishop's Bonfire.*)

O'Donnell, Paedar, *There Will Be Another Day*, Dublin: Dolmen Press, 1963.

O'Faolain, Sean, 'The Case of Sean O'Casey,' vol. 22, *Commonweal* (11 Oct. 1935) pp. 577–578.

O'Hegarty, P. S., *A History of Ireland Under the Union*, London: Methuen, 1952.

Oliver, Edith, 'Off Broadway: Pressed Flowers,' vol. 37, *The New Yorker*, 9 Dec. 1961, 1962. (Review of *Red Roses for Me.*)

O'Neill-Barna, Anne, 'O'Casey at 80: More Rebel Than Ever,' *New York Times Magazine*, 27 March 1960, pp. 26, 90–91.

O'Shaughnessy, J., 'O'Casey: Forever Fare Thee Well,' vol. CLXXXIV, *The Nation* (16 March 1957) pp. 237–239.

Parker, R. B., 'Bernard Shaw and Sean O'Casey,' vol. LXXIII, *Queens Quarterly* (1966) pp. 13–34.

Paul-Dubois, L., 'Le theatre Irlandais,' vol. 27, *Revue Deux Mondes* (1 June 1935) pp. 644–652.

Peacock, Ronald, *The Poet in the Theatre*, New York: Harcourt Brace, 1946.

Pearce, Roy Harvey, 'The Poet as Person,' in *Interpretations of American Literature*, ed. Charles Feidelson and Paul Brodkorb, New York: Oxford, 1960, p. 370.

Phelan, Kappo, 'The Stage and Screen,' vol. 50, *Commonweal* (7 Oct. 1949) pp. 631–632. (Review of *The Silver Tassie.*)

Potter, Stephan, 'Plays and Pictures,' vol. 31, *The New Statesman and Nation* (9 March 1946) p. 173. (Review of *Red Roses for Me.*)

Pritchett, V. S., 'Books: *Within the Gates,*' vol. 31, *The New Yorker* (16 April 1955) pp. 147–148.

——: 'Review of Sean O'Casey by David Krause,' vol. 59, *The New Statesman and Nation* (16 April 1960) p. 560.

Raymond, John, ed., *The Baldwin Age*, London: Eyre & Spottiswoode, 1960.

Redfern, James, 'Theatre,' vol. 176, *Spectator* (8 March 1946) p. 244. (Review of *Red Roses for Me.*)

Reid, Alec, 'The Legend of the Green Crow: Observations on Recent Work by and about Sean O'Casey,' vol. III, *Drama Survey* (Spring-Summer 1963) pp. 155–164.

——: 'Riches Scorned,' vol. 2918, *Times Literary Supplement* (31 Jan. 1958) p. 61.

Ritchie, Harry M., 'The Influence of Melodrama on the Early Plays of Sean O'Casey,' vol. V, *Modern Drama* (Dec. 1962) pp. 164–173.

R. J., 'A New Irish Dramatist,' vol. 135, *Spectator* (21 Nov. 1955) pp. 923–924. (Review of *Juno and the Paycock*.)

Robinson, Eric, '*Juno and the Paycock*: An Introduction,' vol. XI, *Use of English* (London) (1959), pp. 111–118.

Robinson, Lennox, *Curtain Up*, London: M. Joseph, 1942.

——: *Ireland's Abbey Theatre, A History*, London: Sedgwick and Jackson, 1951.

Rogoff, Gordon, 'Sean O'Casey's Legacy,' vol. 81, *Commonweal* (23 Oct. 1964) pp. 128–9.

Rollins, Ronald G., 'Dramatic Symbolism in Sean O'Casey's Dublin Trilogy,' vol. IV, *West Virginia University Philological Papers* (1966) pp. 49–56.

——: 'Form and Content in Sean O'Casey's Dublin Trilogy,' vol. VIII, *Modern Drama* (1965) pp. 419–425.

——: 'O'Casey, O'Neill and Expressionism in *The Silver Tassie*,' vol. X, *Bucknell Review* (May 1962) pp. 364–369.

——: 'O'Casey's *Cock-a-Doodle Dandy*,' vol. XXIII, *Explicator* (Sept. 1964) Item 8.

——: 'O'Casey's *The Silver Tassie*,' vol. XX, Explicator (May 1962) Item 62.

——: 'Sean O'Casey's Mental Pilgrimage,' vol. XVII, *Arizona Quarterly* (Winter 1961) pp. 293–302.

Rudin, Seymour, 'Playwright to Critic: Sean O'Casey's Letters to George Jean Nathan,' vol. V, *Massachusetts Review* (Spring 1964) pp. 326–334.

Ryan, Desmond, *Remembering Sion*, London: A. Barker, 1934.

Sheehy, Michael, *Is Ireland Dying*, New York: Taplinger, 1969.

Shiels, George, *The Caretakers*, Dublin: Golden Eagle, 1948.

——: *The New Gossoon*, London: Macmillan, 1936.

——: *The Passing Day*, London: Macmillan, 1937.

——: *Professor Tim and Paul Twyning*, London: Macmillan, 1927.

——: Two Irish Plays: *Mountain Dew and Cartney and Kevney*, London: Macmillan, 1930.

'*The Shadow of a Gunman*,' vol. 43, *Theatre Arts* (Feb. 1959) pp. 22–23.

Shipp, H., '*The Silver Tassie*,' vol. 49, *English Review* (Nov. 1929) p. 639.

Spender, Stephen, 'A Morality Play With No Morals,' vol. 19, *The New Statesman and Nation* (16 March 1940) p. 363 (Review of *The Star Turns Red*.)

Starkie, Walter, 'The Plays of Sean O'Casey,' vol. 104, *Nineteenth Century* (Aug. 1928) pp. 225–236.

Stokes, Sewell, 'New Plays at Last,' vol. 30, *Theatre Arts* (June 1946) pp. 351–358. (Review of *Red Roses for Me*.)

Sullivan, K., 'Jig Into Eternity,' vol. CXCII, *The Nation* (29 April 1961) pp. 375–376.

Sutton, G., '*The Shadow of a Gunman*,' vol. 72, *Bookman* (London) (July 1927) p. 248.

Synge, John Millington, *Complete Works*, New York: Random House, 1935.

Taylor, A. J. P., *English History, 1914–1945*, Oxford: The Clarendon Press, 1965.

Trewin, J. C., 'Lord of Language,' vol. 35, *Drama* (Winter 1954) pp. 34–38.

Tynan, Kenneth, 'The Trouble in the Studio,' vol. 34, *The New Yorker* (6 Dec. 1958) p. 113. (Review of *The Shadow of a Gunman*.)

Ussher, Arland, *The Face and Mind of Ireland*, London: Gollancz, 1949.

——: *Three Great Irishmen*, London: Gollancz, 1952.

Vansergh, Nicholas, *The Irish Question*, London: George Allen and Unwin, 1958.

Vernon, Grenville, 'The Play,' vol. 21, *Commonweal* (23 Nov. 1934) p. 127. (Review of *The Plough and the Stars*.)

——: 'The Play and Screen,' vol. 21, *Commonweal* (9 Nov. 1934) p. 66. (Review of *Within the Gates*.)

——: 'The Stage and Screen,' vol. 31, *Commonweal* (2 Feb. 1940) p. 327. (Review of *Juno and the Paycock*.)

Waldman, M., '*Juno and the Paycock*,' vol. 13, *The London Mercury* (Feb. 1926) pp. 422–423.

——: '*The Plough and the Stars*,' vol. 14, *The London Mercury* (July 1926) pp. 299–300.

Weales, Gerald, 'Toast to Life,' vol. 19, *Commentary* (Feb. 1955) pp. 201–202.

Williams, Desmond, ed., *The Irish Struggle 1916–26*, London: Routledge & Kegan Paul, 1968.

Worth, Katharine J., 'O'Casey's Dramatic Symbolism,' vol. IV, *Modern Drama* (Dec. 1961) pp. 260–267.

White, Jack, 'Theatre,' vol. 194, *Spectator* (4 March 1955) p. 256. (Review of *The Bishop's Bonfire*.)

Woodbridge, H. E., 'Sean O'Casey,' vol. 40, *The South Atlantic Quarterly* (Jan. 1941) pp. 50–59.

Yeats, William Butler, *The Autobiographies*, New York: Macmillan, 1953.

——: *Collected Plays*, New York: Macmillan, 1952.

Young, Stark, 'Sean O'Casey and Victor Chevkin,' vol. LXI, *The New Republic* (27 Nov. 1929) pp. 17–18. (Review of *The Silver Tassie*.)

——: 'Theatre,' vol. CXVI, *The New Republic* (6 Jan. 1947) p. 42. (Review of *A Pound on Demand*.)

——: 'Theatre,' vol. LXXX, *The New Republic* (7 Nov. 1934) p. 369. (Review of *Within the Gates*.)

Zabel, Morton D., vol. 45, *Poetry* (Dec. 1934) pp. 152–158.

OTHER MERCIER TITLES

IRISH POETS IN ENGLISH *edited by Sean Lucy*
This series of Thomas Davis Lectures gives an account
of Anglo-Irish poetry from its beginnings to the present
day and explores in various ways the different qualities
and the different influences which give it interest and
excellence.

85342 301 6   240pp.   £1.25

THE SHORT STORY *by Sean O'Faolain*
Twenty-four years after it first appeared, Sean
O'Faolain's *The Short Story* is acknowledged not only
as an important critical work in an area that, with the
exception of Frank O'Connor's *The Lonely Voice,* is
singularly barren, but also as one of the most sensitive
studies of the creative process ever written.

85342 302 4   269pp.   £1.05

THE STORY OF ANGLO-IRISH POETRY 1800–
1922 *by Patrick C. Power*
'The author takes the Anglo-Irish poets one by one and
puts them under a magnifying glass to ensure that he
does not miss even the faintest colours that they
borrowed from Gaelic'. *Statesman*
85342 148 X   187pp.   50p

A LITERARY HISTORY OF IRELAND
by Patrick C. Power
The strength of this new guide to Irish writing lies
especially in the fact that it does not seek to view Irish
or Anglo-Irish literature as the only one true literary
expression of the Irish people; both together belong to
Ireland, arose out of Ireland and represent what is
essentially Irish.

85342 149 8   191pp.   75p